Supply is spirit and it is within you. It is never visible and it will never become visible. It is invisible to human eyes; it is never felt with human fingers; it is never heard or tasted. What you behold in the outer world are the forms that supply assumes. Outwardly supply takes the form of money, food, clothing, housing, transportation, business capital, and so forth. Your spiritual discernment will tell you that this is true. Later you will see the proof of it—not by ever seeing supply but by seeing the forms that supply assumes.

Supply is infinite and it is omnipresent wherever you may be. Like Moses, we can realize that we do not have to live on yesterday's manna, nor do we have to gather today's manna for tomorrow; the supply is infinite.

Truth, like supply, is invisible and inaudible. You will never see Truth nor will you ever hear Truth. Truth is within you. Truth is spirit, and Truth is God. What you read in a book or what you hear with your ears are merely symbols of Truth.

INVISIBLE
SUPPLY

INVISIBLE
SUPPLY

Finding the Gifts of the Spirit Within

JOEL S. GOLDSMITH

HarperSanFrancisco
A Division of HarperCollins*Publishers*

All quotations from the Bible are taken from the King James Version.

INVISIBLE SUPPLY: *Finding the Gifts of the Spirit Within.* Copyright © 1983, 1992, 1994 by Geri McDonald, Executrix of The Estate of Joel S. Goldsmith. All rights reserved. Printed in the United States of America. No part of this book may be used or reproduced in any manner whatsoever without written permission except in the case of brief quotations embodied in critical articles and reviews. For information address HarperCollins Publishers, 10 East 53rd Street, New York, NY 10022.

FIRST HARPERCOLLINS PAPERBACK EDITION PUBLISHED IN 1994

ISBN 0-06-250277-8 (pbk)

An Earlier Edition of This Book Was Cataloged As Follows:

Goldsmith, Joel S.

Invisible supply: finding the gifts of the spirit within / Joel S. Goldsmith.—1st ed.

p. cm.

ISBN 0-06-250360-X (alk. paper)

1. Spiritual life. 2. Gifts. I. Title.

BL624.G635   1991   91-41390

234.13—dc20   CIP

02 ❖ HAD 10 9

Except the Lord build the house, they
labor in vain that build it.
—Psalm 127

Illumination dissolves all material ties and binds men
together with the golden chains of spiritual understanding;
it acknowledges only the leadership of the Christ; it has no
ritual or rule but the divine, impersonal universal Love; no
other worship than the inner Flame that is ever lit at the
shrine of Spirit. This union is the free state of spiritual
brotherhood. The only restraint is the discipline of Soul,
therefore we know liberty without license; we are a united
universe without physical limits; a divine service to God
without ceremony or creed. The illumined walk without
fear—by Grace.

—THE INFINITE WAY

CONTENTS

INVISIBLE
SUPPLY

CHAPTER 1

THE PRINCIPLE OF SUPPLY

Webster's *Dictionary* gives the word *principle* as a synonym for God, and Christian Science uses it as such. However, in The Infinite Way we use the word *principle* to mean specifically the principles of life upon which our work and our consciousness are founded. We need principles from which to work and upon which to stand if we are to rise above blind faith as we must.

There are principles in every business, in every art, every profession, and every line of work. Those who abide by these principles, even though they may have many struggles, eventually achieve success.

In our work it is more so. We need principles with which to work because we are continuously faced with appearances of discord, that is, sin, disease in every form, old age, death itself, lack, limitation, and poverty. The Bible tells us that we will have the poor with us always, and we certainly will have them until the principle of supply is understood, and we will have sickness until the principle of health is understood.

Why We Experience Lack

The Infinite Way principle of supply is that in our oneness with God, we already have all that the Father has because "I and the Father are one and all that the Father has is mine." If we individually are experiencing a lack, it is not because of any actual lack. It is because of our inability to make contact with our supply.

In my writings you have seen the reminder that throughout the Great Depression there was no lack in this country. If anything, there was a greater abundance than ever before. Certainly there was a greater abundance of crops, of fish in the oceans, birds in the air, lumber in the forests, grains in warehouses, in barns, and in fields and gardens. This great abundance was not only omnipresent in God; it was actually omnipresent in storehouses and warehouses, in barns and in fields. There was no lack! If any of us suffered from a lack or insufficiency, it was not because there was an actual condition of lack. It was because we were not in tune with the source of supply; we did not have access to the infinite supply.

Therefore, in our work we say, "If you had known the principle of supply, you would not have been in lack or limitation or want during those years." Since there was no actual shortage, any sense of lack was merely an ignorance of the principle of supply.

The principle of supply is the realization that we already have, even though appearances may not testify to that. Because I and the Father are one and all that the Father has is mine, we have. "Son, thou art ever with me, and all that I have is thine."[1] As a child of God you are joint heir with Christ in all the heavenly riches of the Father. That is a spiritual truth given to human consciousness.

Invisible Supply

The world seeks its good in the external realm. It seeks to find peace, joy, satisfaction, home, companionship, or supply from the outer world of people and things. But the Master said, "My kingdom is not of this world."[2] When you turn to the spiritual path, you learn that the world's weapons will not do for us, the world's manner of protecting itself will not do for us, the world's way of seeking its good will not do for us. When you ponder the statement, "The Kingdom of God is within you," it immediately becomes clear that going outside to find your good will not work. The place to seek it is within. The spiritual revelators of all time agree on this.

Spiritual living is based on the ability to contact God. Let it be understood once and for all that there is a God. Not only is there a God but He is at hand. Our mystical poet tells us that He is closer than breathing, nearer than hands and feet. The Master tells us that the Kingdom of this God is within us.

If we are not experiencing life eternal, if we are not having the harmonies, peace, and prosperity to which we are entitled as children of God, let us be fair about it and acknowledge that we have not made His acquaintance, we do not know Him aright. "Acquaint now thyself with him

---

[1]Luke 15:31.
[2]John 18:36.

and be at peace: thereby good shall come unto thee."[3] He shall direct thy paths and you will be at peace. We have not become acquainted with Him. To know Him aright is to have all our ways directed and to be kept in peace. It is really and truly to receive the blessing of life eternal, life harmonious—the good life.

In my early years in this work success came to me quickly and with it prosperity. Then I moved to another city and took upon myself larger obligations. Outwardly it seemed as if I had made a mistake because while I continued to be very successful in healing work, I was unsuccessful in demonstrating supply. I faced a severe lack and limitation in maintaining a family with an insufficient income. I was doing beautiful healing work, being engaged in it all day and all night, and yet I did not have a sufficient return to support my family and myself. It puzzled me because for two years I had been in the work, had demonstrated beyond question that not only were healings taking place, but also supply was being met for others, and yet here was this personal problem of mine. One day the problem became acute.

It probably was not necessary for me to eat or drink or be clothed, but it was necessary for the sake of those who were trusting in my understanding that I know how to accomplish it, why it is accomplished, and when it is accomplished. I had no rest until I found the answers.

One day as I was walking along, the thought came to me that if I really knew God I would not have this problem. I really believed the Bible verse that says, "I have never seen a righteous man begging bread."[4] There could

---

[3]Job 22:21.
[4]Adapted from Psalm 37:25.

be no fault with God or Truth; therefore, the fault must lie with me. Evidently I was not righteous in that sense. Evidently I did not have the right idea of supply. Something surely was wrong.

The unfoldment was clear. My lack of understanding of God was responsible for my situation. At first glance it seems impossible that a person could be actively engaged in spiritual work and bringing about actual healings and still not know God, not have the correct understanding of God. But I thought, "It must be so. Scripture is true. The fault is entirely with me. Evidently I do not know God." I could put this to the test and see whether or not I knew God.

I asked myself, "What is God?" I began to give all the answers that would probably occur to you. However, I soon realized that the answers could not be Truth because they were not of my own knowledge. I was merely quoting, "God is love." John said that; I did not *know* it. "God is law." I suppose it was Moses who said that, but I did not *know* it. Mrs. Eddy said, "God is principle." But I did not *know* that. I realized that the things I knew about God were not true knowledge of God; they were mere quotations about God, things that others knew about God, not things that I *knew*. I knew nothing but quotations; I did not know God.

Knowing statements of truth about God and knowing God are different things. I pondered then on what is God and what do I know about God. No answer came. Then I began to think about humanity, what humanity is, what I am. I realized that God is the *I* of my being, the *I am*—not my humanhood, not my personal mind or power or understanding—the *I am* of me, the very *I* or spiritual selfhood of me. God constitutes the *I* that I am. God is the

I that I am. God is the very life, the very soul, the mind, the consciousness of individuals. If that is true, then all that God has is part of each human being. All that the Father hath is mine. All of the God-mind is the human mind. All of the God-soul is the human soul. All of God's spirit is the human spirit. All of God's supply is the human supply. All of God's love is human love. Why? Because *I* and the Father are one and all that the Father hath is mine. It is that oneness that constitutes the infinity of our being. In and of ourselves we would be nothing. But since God constitutes our real being, since God is the Father of our real being, then God has established in us the fullness of His wisdom, the fullness of His love, the fullness of His life, the fullness of His supply. "The earth is the Lord's, and the fullness thereof,"[5] and "Son, all that I have is thine."[6]

The realization came that since this Allness constitutes individual being, our good does not come to us from outside; it has to be contacted from inside. That immediately changed my understanding and it changed my life.

As you know, God has a way of meeting our need at every level; soon thereafter I came across a poem by Robert Browning in which he states that we must not try to open an entry for good to come into us from the without, but rather we must open out a way for the imprisoned splendor within us to escape. In other words, all of the good, all of eternality and immortality, all of Godhood, all of Christhood, all of spirituality is embodied within us, but we must open out a way for the imprisoned splendor to escape.

---

[5]Psalm 24:1.
[6]Luke 15:31.

Watch the miracle take place as you realize that this splendor of God, this infinite love, this infinite life, this divine wisdom, this spiritual grace, the Comforter, is already within you. This splendor of God that multiplies loaves and fishes, that heals the sick and preaches the gospel to the poor, that opens the eyes of the blind, is already within you. You no longer look outside to persons.

A spouse immediately loses the feeling of dependence on the loved one; a businessperson immediately loses the feeling of dependence on position, investments, or business. You come to the realization that even though supply may come *through* these channels, the *source* of supply is within oneself. In that realization new and better avenues open. Should one avenue be closed, you gain confidence that others will open as the need arises.

Supply Is Spirit

Supply is spirit and it is within you. It is never visible and it will never become visible. It is invisible to human eyes; it is never felt with human fingers; it is never heard or tasted. What you behold in the outer world are the forms that supply assumes. Outwardly supply takes the form of money, food, clothing, housing, transportation, business capital, and so forth. Your spiritual discernment will tell you that this is true. Later you will see the proof of it—not by ever seeing supply, but by seeing the forms that supply assumes.

Supply is infinite and it is omnipresent wherever you may be. Like Moses, we can realize that we do not have to live on yesterday's manna, nor do we have to gather today's manna for tomorrow; the supply is infinite.

Truth, like supply, is invisible and inaudible. You will never see Truth, nor will you ever hear Truth. Truth is within you. Truth is spirit, and Truth is God. What you read in a book or what you hear with your ear are merely symbols of Truth.

Tangibles and Intangibles; the Visible and Invisible

The fruit on trees and crops in the fields are symbols of supply. They are not supply itself, because supply is invisible and it is within you. In my book *The Infinite Way* I illustrate this principle by an orange tree. Oranges, even to an orange grower, are not supply, because when the oranges have been harvested and sold or the wind has blown them away or for some reason the crop must be destroyed, the supply is still there. Supply is operating inside of the tree and will appear in its due season as another crop of oranges. When that crop is removed, the supply still has not been used up because supply will appear next season in another crop as a form of supply.

Wars and depressions have deprived many people of their wealth or abundance, and they have experienced lack and limitation, sometimes total lack. But some were able to reestablish themselves, some to a greater extent than before, because although they lost their money, they did not lose their ability to earn more. They had not lost their supply. They still had the intelligence, energy, ideas, or inspiration that created their original wealth. Ideas, inspiration, intelligence, wisdom, service, or love bring about the forms of supply, but they themselves are invisible. Only the results are visible.

When a business is being sold, often goodwill is listed as an asset. I know of one business that sold its assets for a half million dollars but its goodwill for one million dollars. The intangible goodwill was worth more than the physical assets of the company. No one can ever see, hear, taste, touch, or smell goodwill. It is an intangible.

So it is with all poets, authors, sculptors, painters, composers. Their invisible talents are the substance of what becomes visible as poems, books, paintings, teachings, or other forms of art. Their supply is their inner light, their inspiration.

Supply Is Embodied in Us

The error of most religious teachings is in the belief that supply is something that comes to us, and a great deal of time is wasted in praying for it to be given to us.

We know that such spiritual qualities as integrity, loyalty, morality, honesty, and charity are embodied in our consciousness. We do not pray for these qualities to be added to us; they are qualities that we express. Whether or not we express them to the fullest of our understanding is another question.

Supply is just as spiritual as such qualities. It too is not something that comes to us; it is embodied within us and we must express it. This we do by casting our "bread" upon the waters, and it comes back to us as our supply. This is the only supply to which we are spiritually entitled. We are not permitted to take someone else's supply. Prisons are full of people who tried to take the bread that someone else had placed on the waters.

Casting Bread upon the Water

The Master gave us many examples of how we may cast our bread upon the waters: forgiving, praying for our enemies, sharing, and tithing.

Forgiving and Praying for Our Enemies

Christ Jesus tells us to forgive seventy times seven those who in any way offend us. He tells us to pray for our enemies, for those who despitefully use us, for those who persecute us. This is not limited to those who offend us personally. Remember that if they offend my neighbor, they offend me. If they offend my country, they offend me. If they offend my race, they offend me. In the last analysis, if they offend this world at all, they offend me because we are all parts of one whole. Since there is only one God who is the Father of us all, we are brothers and sisters; whoever offends one of us offends all of us. So it is, then, that we are called upon under this law of Christ to forgive those who offend us, persecute us, and abuse us.

We are to pray for our enemies even more than for our friends. The Master tells us that it profits us nothing to pray for our friends. We must also pray for our enemies in order to be the children of God; and as children of God, we are heirs of God, joint heirs with Christ to all the supply that heaven holds. You become an heir to the heavenly riches that God has to bestow only when you learn to pray for your enemies and for humankind's enemies and learn to forgive those who offend you. Even if they offend you four hundred and eighty-nine times, you are to forgive seventy times seven (four hundred and ninety times). Forgiving others and praying for your enemies are two of the ways in which we can demonstrate our spiritual supply.

Sharing

Verily I say unto you, Inasmuch as ye have done it unto one of the least of these my brethren, ye have done it unto me. [7]

The good you do to another, you are doing to yourself. There is but one selfhood. There is but one God and therefore but one life. Therefore, my life is your life. The same life that courses in my veins is coursing in yours. The same intelligence that is manifest in me is manifest in you. The same soul that animates my being animates your being. There is only one *I. I* is God, and that God constitutes my being. It is my life and your life because there is only one life. God is my mind and your mind, because there is only one mind. God is my soul and your soul. We have the same soul. We have the same soul, the same life, the same spirit, and the same being. Therefore, the good you do to another, you are doing unto God, who is your divine selfhood. The good you do to another, you do to yourself.

In other words, when we mail a check to any philanthropy, benevolence, or charity, it is like mailing it to our own bank account. It may take a week or two to return to our bank account, but it will get there because we have mailed it to ourselves.

Whatever you do to another, you are doing unto God, your divine selfhood. The harm you do to another, you are doing to yourself because there is only one self. You cannot

----

[7]Matthew 25:40.

hurt any self without hurting yourself. An injustice or an injury that we do to another, we do to ourselves.

No one is to blame for our problems but ourselves. We create our own karma. That is, the good we do today eventually returns to us as good. The evil we do today eventually returns to us as evil. We create our own future every moment that we live because there is only one self and whatever we do, we are doing unto ourselves.

Gratitude

Another way to "cast our bread upon the waters" is by expressing gratitude, which can take many forms. Most of the charity that is done in this world, regardless of what form it takes, is probably done because of gratitude. Someone is grateful for something and sends a check to C.A.R.E. or to the Tuberculosis Foundation or the Cancer Society or to some other favorite charity. As a rule, a sense of gratitude prompts these acts of benevolence.

Gratitude has still another form. To me the highest expression of gratitude is the realization that God is the invisible source of all that is visible and that He is responsible for all of the good on this earth and on all the other planets. I doubt that I could ever bring myself to thank God for anything that I have or that comes to me, probably because I do not believe in a God who provides only for me or sends only to me. I do not believe God created sunshine or rain or the cattle on a thousand hills especially for me. I believe that all of these exist as God's expression of His own infinite being, of His own infinite abundance, spread forth for all the sons and daughters of God and not only for a favored few.

Being grateful for the fish in the sea, the birds in the air, the cattle on a thousand hills, the trees that bloom, for all that we witness from waking until sleeping, for the fact that the principle of life is at work for us even while we are sleeping is to me the highest form of gratitude, because there is nothing personal in it. It is a sense of gratitude that the the infinity of God is omnipresent for all of us to share.

The fact that so few receive from this infinite abundance has nothing at all to do with God. There is no favoritism on the part of God. God does not give more to one than to another. God has no favorite children, no favorite race, no favorite nation, nor does God reward the virtuous and punish the sinful. It is difficult to accept the doctrine of God's rewarding the virtuous and punishing the sinful when one sees so many sweet, virtuous people suffering disease or lack while so many rascals abound in health and supply.

Our supply is in direct proportion to our receptivity; that is, the degree of gratitude that we express, the degree of bread that we place upon the waters in the form of benevolence, forgiveness, praying for our enemies, and so forth demonstrates our receptivity, because then we are expressing the spiritual principle of supply.

Tithing

Years ago gratitude was expressed by tithing to the church, the source of spiritual food and spiritual comfort. The church was also often the only source of material help. When tithing was directed to the church from a sense of gratitude for its benevolence, it was a blessing to both the giver and the receiver. However, eventually some shrewd individuals figured out that by giving 10 percent they might get 90 percent in return, and tithing became a percentage deal. Because of this, tithing lost its effectiveness and eventually disappeared as a general custom, although it continued among the Mormons, the Quakers, and some minority groups. But, on the whole, tithing is no longer recognized, as it once was, as a means of expressing gratitude for what we receive from the spiritual source of our lives.

Tithing, when it is practiced anonymously as the Master taught it, is a joy, a pleasure, a privilege to those who have rediscovered it. Those who tithe, without letting anyone know of it and with gratitude as their only motive, discover that there is indeed a Father who rewards openly. "Thy Father which seeth in secret . . . shall reward thee openly."[8] But one must not tithe for the reward, for then it becomes a business proposition and is no longer a spiritual activity.

These days the church is no longer the only avenue of benevolence. For those in need, material help is now available from a multitude of charitable institutions, foundations, medical associations, hospitals, orphanages, schools for the handicapped, and homes for the aged, as well as from city, county, state, and federal programs. Therefore, tithing can now be directed not only to our spiritual source but also to these other benevolent sources. In this way, we prove that we love our neighbor as ourselves, and our neighbors are the people of all religions, races, and creeds, not only those of our religious households. We are not looking for supply to come to us; we are proving that we have supply, even if it is expressed in only pennies or pence.

---

[8]Matthew 6:4.

Jesus . . . beheld how the people cast money into
the treasury: and many that were rich cast in much.
And there came a certain poor widow, and she threw
in two mites, which make a farthing. And He . . .
saith unto them . . . This poor widow hath cast more
in, than all they which have cast into the treasury:
for all they did cast in of their abundance; but she of
her want did cast in all that she had, even all her
living. [9]

Some people give away great fortunes yet are no more blessed than the widow who gave the mite. What matters is not the number of pounds or dollars you give; it is the amount you give in proportion to your immediate means. In dollars and cents or in pounds and pence it is impossible to measure how much we should give. The only measuring stick is how much love we are expressing, how much cooperation, how much recognition, how much praying, how much forgiving, how much we give in secrecy without drawing the attention of others to our benevolence.

Demonstrating Supply

Understanding the difference between supply and the forms of supply is one of the most practical lessons you will ever learn in life. When you understand this principle, you will stop trying to demonstrate the forms of supply and you will find yourself in possession of abundance. Why? The forms of supply are not permanent. When the forms have been used up, you have to do the work all over again. Demonstrating a fresh supply of forms every week of every month is extremely laborious, and it is not necessary.

---

[9] Mark 12:41–44.

When you demonstrate spiritual supply, the forms of supply roll on forever, and you never again have to take thought for what you shall eat or what you shall drink or wherewithal you shall be clothed. Demonstrate spiritual supply once and for all, then let that supply appear outwardly in whatever forms it chooses.

To demonstrate spiritual supply, all you have to demonstrate is God, by recognizing that supply is God or God is supply. You have to demonstrate the realization of God within you, the consciousness of God, the awareness of God's Presence. Once you have done that, the rest automatically follows. Every year in due season a new crop appears. Every time new shoes are needed, they appear. Every time a new automobile is needed, it appears. Every time the rent is due, it appears. Why? Because you have demonstrated *Infinite* supply.

In The Infinite Way there is but one demonstration to make: the realization of your own consciousness. You cannot make that demonstration anywhere outside of your own consciousness. It is not an experience external to you. It is an experience that takes place within your own consciousness.

Demonstrate the realization of God as the Source and Fount of all supply, and, having God, you have all that belongs to God. "Son, thou art ever with me and all that I have is thine." As long as you are with God and as long as you have God with you, you have supply. It will appear externally as health, money, transportation, or whatever else you need.

CHAPTER 2

SECRECY, THE PRIMAL
MYSTICAL PRINCIPLE

Secrecy is one of the greatest positive powers ever turned loose in the world. You will find the principle of secrecy mentioned in many of my writings, but now I am giving it to you with full force because everything is based on this principle. Without secrecy you may as well give up hope of making progress, because the moment you violate spiritual secrecy, you lose God.

Spiritual Secrecy

In the past when we prayed and healings took place or supply was increased, we may have felt that we were doing God a favor by telling all our friends how profitable it was to pray and what good things happened through prayer. Let me tell you that this is the fastest way in the world to lose God!

17

The Master said to the leper whom He had healed,

> See thou say nothing to any man: but go thy way,
> show thyself to the priest. . . .[1]

When I started out on The Infinite Way, if I had said from a platform that for two months I had been undergoing an inner initiation and had been given a message, people would have called me crazy, because few were ready to receive such a message. Only those who had witnessed the fruitage of this message could and did believe, because

> Natural man receiveth not the things of the Spirit
> of God: for they are foolishness unto him: neither
> can he know them, because they are spiritually
> discerned.[2]

If you tell members of your family or your friends or neighbors about a spiritual experience you have had that produced the most wonderful results, you may soon find them avoiding you. You cannot expect them to understand something that they have never experienced or witnessed, because they cannot see through your eyes or know through your mind.

A book may contain the most profound secrets, but you will not appreciate them until the secrets have entered your consciousness to such an extent that you can spiritually discern them. It is much like the old-time pearl divers. Until their consciousness discerned pearls as something of value, the divers did not need to be watched or the pearls guarded. It was also true of the early diamond miners. The value of the pearls and diamonds had to enter

---

[1] Mark 1:44.
[2] 1 Corinthians 2:14.

the consciousness of the divers and miners before they wanted to own them.

There are secrets in my book *The Thunder of Silence* that have been revealed to fewer than one reader in a hundred, because the secrets have not yet come into the range of most readers' experience.

That is why I tell you to keep every spiritual experience locked up within yourself. When you try to reveal such secrets, you come up against the brick wall of somebody's disbelief.

Keep secret and sacred every spiritual experience that you have, even the demonstrations of harmony, healing, or supply that may come as the fruitage. Do not give testimonies about them. Do not tell them to your friends or relatives if you can avoid it. Try to act as if your demonstrations were just the natural thing and not some kind of miracle that took place as the result of a treatment or prayer. We do not need to advertise our healings or our demonstrations, because God will shout them from the housetops in the consciousness of those who are ready to understand. It would do others no good at all to know of them.

As you attain some measure of God-awareness and as you hold it secret and sacred within you, you will become a silent influence in all the congresses of the world. You will not become famous, nor will the world build monuments to you, but, in your own silent way, you will be contributing to the health and harmony of your family, of your friends, of your relatives, of your community, and ultimately of the entire world. But you will do so only by maintaining secrecy based on the knowledge that what you experience is sacred. Hold it within yourself!

What We May Share and with Whom

As you begin to show forth the fruitage of spiritual living, many will come to you asking what is this truth that you have. But they do not really want to know this truth; what they want to have is the fruitage! All Pilate wanted to know was how to multiply loaves and fishes, heal the sick, and influence multitudes. You will find that many have their eyes on the fruit, not on the principle. Then you had better turn and walk away, because if you are not spiritually wise and blurt out the secret, they will say, "Oh, I've heard about that. It's nonsense!" Then you will be left with an empty feeling as if you have given away a pearl of great price, which was not accepted, and as if you have lost it and now have less than you had before.

Be satisfied to share the "milk," the most easily digested spiritual food. Share books or tapes or gentle statements of Truth, and give healings to the fullest extent that you can. This we do share and we should share liberally. We may share the letter of Truth, the principle of Truth, but not our experiences. Let each one have his or her own experiences.

As others come seeking the Truth, treat them as you were treated. Give them a book or recommend one. Let them, through their own efforts, also move easily, gently, gradually through the letter of Truth, because the greatest mistake of the metaphysical and spiritual world is believing that you can help others into heaven. In my thirty-two years of experience I have discovered that those who had the capacity to attain spiritual Truth did attain it. Their association with me in this message helped, but it was not I who did it and it was not The Infinite Way that did it. It was their receptivity to the message of The Infinite Way that led them to Truth. Those who did not have the capacity did not attain it even when I spent days, weeks, and months pouring the message into them. All I could accomplish was to strike the match and light the bonfire of their spiritual hopes if they had already laid the firewood. Because I have been lifted up, I was able to lift them up partway. But it was their receptivity to the message and their developing spiritual capacity that attained it.

Therefore, let us share the "milk" while keeping our spiritual experiences locked up within us.

There is one exception to that rule. If you have a really knowing practitioner who shows forth spiritual life, do not hestitate to share your spiritual experiences with him or her. When you share with your practitioner, you are pouring your spiritual treasures into his or her secrecy and they are being received and welcomed, and your practitioner can increase them for you. The deeper and further you go, the greater will be the revelations your practitioner will give you, because then you will have the capacity of secrecy to receive them and embody them and hold them as if they were seeds planted in the ground.

If you remain on this path, you will inevitably have spiritual experiences. You will tabernacle with God within you; you will witness the Spirit of Christ in some experiences; you will receive Truths in consciousness; you will hear the still, small voice. But when you do, do not advertise it. Do not try to convince anyone. Do not think you can save anyone by telling them of your wonderful experiences, because they will make mockery of you. At best, they will challenge you to "remove a lump" or heal them in some way, and you will wonder if that is all they got out of what you said. Their response will show the shallowness of their understanding.

Remember that the first and most important principle of the mystical life is secrecy. Keep locked up within you what you know and what you experience. Let it remain within you as though it were a seed planted in the ground. Nourish it, let it come to fruitage, and then share of the fruitage.

Pray in Secret

The Master stressed secrecy in praying. From the very start of the Sermon on the Mount He taught that we are to do our praying in secret. We are not to pray to be seen by others. He told us that those who do pray openly receive a benefit from other people but lose the benefit that accrues from God. This is important to remember. We have a choice to make. Do we want human approval more than the grace of God?

Do not pray where you can be seen by others so that you will receive their approval. In small communities especially, those who attend church regularly are known as good Christians. But the Master said that by gaining the approbation of your neighbor, you lose the Grace of God. And you do! That is one of the reasons why prayers are rarely answered. We are violating the terms of prayer. Let us see why this is so.

What is the source of answered prayer? If you were to pray in the middle of a group meeting, from what direction would you expect an answer? From the other people sitting in the room, or from God? Is it not clear that you do not expect an answer to your prayer from any of your companions? They might think you are a good Christian if they see you at prayer, but that does not in any way answer your prayer. From what direction is your prayer answered?

From God! Where is God? God is within you, but where were you when you were praying? You were out in the middle of the room, and your prayer never reached the throne of God. It reached only as high as the approval of those sitting around you watching you pray. Your mind was not on God when you were praying.

In order for your mind to be on God, you have to be far away from the influence of any gathering of people. You have to dwell in the sanctuary of your own being where you cannot be interrupted by a telephone or distracted by the sight or sound of people around you or even the perfume they may be wearing. If you want to commune with God, you must be so alone that you could not even hear a cry for help if it came to you. You must shut out the entire world. God is closer to you than breathing and nearer than hands and feet, but God is hidden within you.

If you hope to break through the veil of illusion, of superstition, of ignorance of God, of worship of false gods, you must get away somewhere—under the stars or under the trees or in your room—where you can be so alone with God that you will not even hear the birds singing. When you enter your inner sanctuary—closing your door, shutting off your senses, shutting out the world—and get inside yourself in secret, then the Father who sees in secret will reward you openly.

The principle of secrecy in prayer and almsgiving is one of the forgotten secrets. The entire world is violating that principle. Churches ignore this principle, but the words of the Master in the New Testament will stay forever and cannot be ignored.

Once you learn the nature of secrecy, you will understand that if God is with us and for us, it really makes no difference if the whole world is against us. It makes no difference what anybody's opinion of us is if we have the good opinion of the Father who sees in secret.

There is no need to wear a sanctimonious face to make others think you are virtuous or righteous. It is not their business. Your relationship with God is no one's business. It is your business alone that you are so at one with God that you live in accord with His laws and would not violate them. Therefore, as the Master taught, do not do as the hyprocrites did. Do not wear sackcloth and ashes and pray out on the street corner to be seen by others and appear sanctimonious to them. Do not do any of these things. Just wear your usual clothing and look bright and cheerful and normal and keep your relationship with God a secret.

Give Alms in Secret

When we want to go to God in earnest, when we really want to pray, the one thing that we require above all is privacy, quietness, solitude—an atmosphere of peace. The last thing we want is a witness. Our prayers, our benevolences, and our inner communions are so sacred that they must be kept secret. Never believe that your benevolences and charities are of any value to you if anyone knows about them. You may see in newspaper columns the names of those who contributed to this or that charity. These benevolences are a blessing to those who benefit from the contributions, but the donors are not benefiting. Be assured of that! This is a spiritual principle!

Giving is a form of prayer because this is doing unto others as we would have them do unto us. It is loving our neighbors as ourselves, and therefore it is prayer. The prayer of benevolence, charity, giving, helpfulness is sacred. Being sacred, it must be secret. It must be

something between the Father and you, because whatever
you give is not your own. It is God's. Remember that the
earth is the Lord's and the fullness thereof—not yours.
You may be the custodian at this moment of one dollar or
one million, but it is not yours! Therefore, in your giving,
you are merely acting as an agent for the Father, and the
Father wants no publicity because the Father's love is
universal, impersonal, and impartial. Giving must be in
secret. It must be as secret as praying, and praying must
never be done before the world.

Wanting to help someone is about the noblest motive
there is, but there is nothing noble in giving and letting it
be known by anyone but God. Your supply was given to
you by an act of Grace, and it is your privilege to share it to
any extent you like. But if you help someone, it is between
you and your heart and God. It is of no concern to anyone
but you and your Father who provided the means with
which to help. Is it anybody's business but yours and God's
that you are helping someone? Is it loving to those in need
to tell the world that they needed and accepted charity?
They may be embarrassed or feel demeaned to have their
neighbor or community made aware that they are desti-
tute.

Publicizing your acts of benevolence has every sem-
blance of your wanting to be well thought of by the public,
and you will forfeit God's Grace. Give your alms secretly
and the Father who sees in secret will reward you openly.

When you have a need, always remember that "your
Father knoweth what things ye have need of."[3] Who is
better able to give it to you than God? You do not have
to tell anyone, hoping that if you tell enough people,

---

[3]Matthew 6:8.

someone will help you. If we keep our needs locked up secretly within ourselves, before long the fulfillment comes, because the Father within us, who sees in secret, rewards openly.

Virtues Are Shouted from the Housetops

As you hold "I and my Father are one" in sacredness and secrecy within yourself, remember that it also means that "I and my neighbor are one," because we are children of the same Father. We are branches of the same tree. We are united in the tree of life. When you abide in this within yourself, you will never have to voice it. It will be shouted from the housetops that love, compassion, helpfulness, mutuality, and cooperation govern your relationships with others.

It is the same thing as being honest or moral. You do not have to tell anyone that you are honest or moral because, as Emerson tells us, "What you are shrieks so loudly I cannot hear what you say." Therefore, if there is integrity in us, let us not tell each other about it. Let the other person find it out. If there is mortality in us, let us not tell anyone about it; let them find out for themselves. If there is charity or forgiveness in us, let us not tell anyone about it. Let them find out about it. By our very secrecy, God will in some way make our character known to the world. We will never have to voice it, and we will have the benefit that accrues to us from holding within ourselves our secret good and our relationship with God.

One of the evils of talking is that we "leak" our good. It is as if you had invented something and told everybody about it and by the time you applied for a patent, someone else would have already patented it. It is like the woman who waited months for the sales to buy a heavy winter coat with fur trimming at half price. When the coats were on sale, she immediately phoned her friends and relatives to tell them about it. When she went to the store, she found that the coats had all been sold.

Our outer experience is the externalization of our state of consciousness. We do not have to talk about what is going on in our consciousness; the mere fact that it is happening will externalize itself. In other words, if you are living morning, noon, and night in the realization that "I and my Father are one, and I am ever with my Father, and all that the Father has is mine"; if you abide in that truth and keep it locked up in you, eventually others will see that it is absolutely true. It would be foolish to tell it to anyone, because no one would believe it. What is locked up in us in the form of consciousness is outwardly evident. We do not need to voice it.

Let us begin to live in the realization that the Kingdom of God is within us and do all of our communing with God within ourselves in secrecy.

Let us ignore "man whose breath is in his nostrils: for wherein is he to be accounted of?"[4]

Live your inner life in secret contemplation with the Father. You are now living at one with the vine, with the Christ who is within you. Live your life wholly in an inner communion with God by shutting off the outer avenues and channels, and begin to draw your good from the withinness.

> Put not your trust in princes, nor in the son of man, in whom there is no help.[5]

---

[4]Isaiah 2:22.
[5]Psalm 146:3.

CHAPTER 3

THE PRINCIPLE OF
CONTEMPLATIVE MEDITATION

Most religious teachings tell us that the Spirit of the Lord is everywhere. If that were true, everybody would be free, healthy, wealthy, independent, joyous, and harmonious, and there would be no slavery, bondage, lack, or limitation. But that is not the condition of the world, so that teaching cannot be true.

It is like saying that electricity is everywhere. However, until it is connected to your particular use, it does you no good. So it is with the Spirit of the Lord. In an absolute spiritual sense, the Spirit of the Lord *is* everywhere; but if you do not realize God, if you do not make contact with God, if you do not feel the actual presence of God, then as far as you are concerned, it is not there. The Infinite Way principle is that the Spirit of the Lord is *only* where it is realized.

God-Realization

The whole secret lies in the word *consciousness*. If you are conscious of the presence of the Lord, if you are conscious of the activity of God, then it is so unto you. To develop this consciousness we meditate or reach out to practitioners for help. Until we ourselves have realized the Spirit of the Lord, we turn to a practitioner who has the capacity (either inborn or developed) to realize God. If you can contact the consciousness of a Jesus Christ or of a John or of a Paul, your troubles are over and harmony is instantly restored to you because you have touched the consciousness of one who has attained God-realization. It makes no difference whether the practitioner is an Infinite Way student, a Christian Science student, or a Unity student as long as the practitioner is of a realized God-consciousness. On the other hand, if the practitioner is *not* of realized God-consciousness, regardless of what teaching he or she follows, you will get no benefit except possibly a little human comfort. You will have no demonstration of health, harmony, wholeness, completeness, or perfection.

The Infinite Way practitioner has every possibility of meeting your need more quickly or surely because of The Infinite Way's advanced teaching on attaining God-consciousness. But the teaching itself will not meet your need. It is the practitioner's degree of attained God-realization or God-consciousness that meets the need. The only value of any truth is in the degree of your realization of it.

Yes, you can find a practitioner to give you help or to give you some particular healing, but be assured that if you do not develop your own spiritual consciousness, you cannot expect your permanent freedom from human ills. The Master made it clear. "If I go not away, the Comforter will not come to you." If I, Joel, make all your demonstrations every day, what happens to you when I leave? The very thing that has happened to many whose practitioners moved away. Do not get caught in that position! It is ye who must know the Truth. Study and practice the principles of The Infinite Way, begin to understand Truth, declare it, live it, and work with it, and make yourself permanently free from human ills.

Our only reason for being on the spiritual path is to build spiritual consciousness. It is true that when we are on the path, we find that most of our human ills disappear and greater harmonies are established in all of our human relationships, but these are not the reason for being on the spiritual path—these are only the added things. But the only way we can successfully overcome the inharmonies, discords, sins, diseases, and ultimately death is through the development of spiritual consciousness.

Spiritual Consciousness

What is spiritual consciousness? Spiritual consciousness is faith and reliance on the Infinite Invisible for all things. Spiritual awareness or consciousness reveals that there is only one God and that there is only one Life, one Love, one Substance, one Law, one Activity, one Cause, and one Effect—every synonym of God that you know.

A material consciousness relies on something in the outer world. For example, a materially minded person says that to go from here to San Francisco is dependent upon having so many dollars. The spiritually minded person says that the trip is dependent upon the Grace of God, which cannot be seen, heard, or touched.

The materially minded person says that aspirin will cure a headache. The spiritually minded person says that health is an activity of God and that the Grace of God is the source of health.

The spiritually minded person knows that what is visible is only an outer manifestation of what is invisible. How did the Bible come into existence except from the invisible consciousness of the saints and prophets who spoke or wrote these words? Out of the invisible came their words into visible, tangible expression—the Bible. But these words will only help you get back into the invisible from which more words begin to flow through you. Living on the printed words alone is living on an effect, on a husk, and you will miss the opportunity to hear more words from the same source. Living in the realization of the invisible as the source of the visible is living on the actual substance of life, for we do not live by bread alone but by every word that proceedeth out of the mouth of God. Bread is not the staff of life; the word of God is the staff of life, those words that flow from the invisible within you to the visible.

The human belief is that if you go to enough stores, you will eventually find a particular item at the right price. That is the human way. The spiritual way is realizing that it cannot be found in a store. It is a gift of God within you; it has already been given to you within and you desire to see it made manifest without. When you realize that it is already established within you in the invisible, in some way or manner you are led to the very store at the very moment it is being put on the counter, and you will find it waiting for you!

Never go to the market for food without realizing that the real substance is within you. Then, when you do your marketing, you will find that the spiritual realization has directed you, and you will save both money and time.

Before undertaking any activity in life, turn to the Source, which is God. The source of everything in the world is God—even a vacation. God is the Source, the Activity, the Substance. Becoming spiritually minded is being reliant and dependent only upon the Infinite Invisible. As we become less and less dependent on the external values of life, we develop our spiritual consciousness. Developing our spiritual consciousness must become the major part of our lives.

As you embody Truth, you become a healer. You may not necessarily become a public practitioner, but you become a practitioner to all those within your circle who desire spiritual healing.

Developing Spiritual Consciousness

We develop spiritual consciousness through the activity of Truth in our consciousness. This is accomplished in two steps.

The first is when, as beginning students, we read and hear and expose ourselves to Truth. The more we read and contemplate scriptural statements and absolutely true metaphysical statements, the more we associate with those on the path, and the more we spiritualize thought—the more we maintain the activity of Truth in our consciousness. All the years that we have spent in reading truth, hearing truth, thinking truth, attending church services or lectures or classes—all those years are fruitful in leading us to the second and more important step, where inspiration flows from within our own being.

Having gone through our initiatory experience of maintaining the activity of Truth in our consciousness, we come to the second stage when, through meditation, we are able to receive Truth from within our own being. At this stage, we no longer think Truth, read it, or hear it with our minds. Instead, we have developed the inner ear and the inner eye and are now aware of the still, small voice and receive impartations of the Word from God. The most important phase of the activity of Truth in consciousness is when truth comes to our consciousness from within our own being. Once this flow starts from within, it really makes no difference if we never see each other again or read another spiritual book or attend another church service or lecture or class, because we get our sufficiency from within our own being. If we wish, we can still attend classes, lectures, or church services. But it is no longer our dependency; it is now for the pleasure of association.

Spiritual Consciousness Through Meditation

The first stage of meditation is when you are pondering, cogitating, or contemplating God and the spiritual universe. For example, "I wonder what God is. I wonder what God's spiritual universe is. I know very little about God, if anything. I wonder what the activity of God would be if we could actually see it or hear it." That is what I mean by pondering or contemplating, and we do this quietly and peacefully. That is the stage and state of meditation that helps us to contact spiritual consciousness.

Meditation in and of itself will not do anything for you except to the degree that it enables you to make your contact with God. In The Infinite Way we meditate many, many times a day for this purpose. We quietly and peacefully contemplate a passage of Scripture such as, "Thy grace is my sufficiency," or "Where the Spirit of the Lord is, there is liberty," or "Man shall not live by bread alone but by every word of God." We contemplate for three, four, or five minutes and then sit for a minute or two in complete quiet and then go about our business. We do not sit there waiting until the contact is realized. During meditation we merely open ourselves to a state of receptivity and then go about our business, because the actual "click" or contact may come ten or twenty minutes later, an hour later, or after a night's sleep.

This morning, after several hours of sleep, as I awakened, I found myself in contact. All of my meditations of yesterday added up, and during the complete relaxation of sleep, contact was realized. And so it will be for you. You may meditate in the morning before starting your day's work, and then an hour later you will suddenly find yourself right in the middle of the Spirit, or it may happen later.

It is not wise to sit in meditation waiting for the contact, because the waiting is apt to be a mental strain, and you will never make contact while there is any such strain. It is only in the moment that thought is still that "the bridegroom cometh." It is only in that moment when there is no mental activity that God-contact is realized. Contact with God does not happen when there is a reasoning, thinking process going on.

An inventor may have a problem and give it much thought and work and yet find no solution. But when he or she completely leaves the problem by going out to play tennis or retiring to sleep or rest, when the inventor's mind is completely distracted, the solution pops right up. In our work it happens the same way. The moment the mind is off the subject, the mind that was also in Christ Jesus is on the field.

In order to make this contact we have frequent periods of meditation and go inside quietly and review and remember and declare within ourselves one or more of these Truths. In this way they become so much a part of our lives that we are really not living so much by bread as we are by the Word of God that is entertained in our consciousness.

It takes a very small statement of Truth to spark our consciousness into action, and it is this activity of Truth in our consciousness that brings about the development of our spiritual consciousness. It is not *what* we read that does it; it is what we *do* with what we read that does it. Far too many students study too much. The study of Truth is the smallest part of our life's demonstration. "Man shall not live by bread alone but by every word that proceedeth out of the mouth of God" is a beautiful statement. But it is only a seed of Truth, and reading it and repeating it does not increase your spiritual consciousness. You must take it into your consciousness and live by it.

You must make it a practice to pause every few minutes, every half hour, or every hour and remember some passage of Truth, some quotation of Scripture, some statement from the textbook you may be studying. Some Word of God must be entertained in your consciousness over and over throughout the day and night. Eventually you will find that you are fed, clothed, and housed by those very passages of Truth more than by the food you eat. You will find that your business is nourished or your talents and abilities are increased—more by the Word of Truth in your consciousness than by any natural ability.

We call this practice *practicing the Presence of God* or *contemplative meditation*. It means that we are contemplating, cogitating, mulling over, or pondering the Word of God and maintaining it in our consciousness. Contemplative meditation primes the spiritual pump, because after only a few months of this type of living, a new experience will come to you. You will find that "in moments when ye think not" a Word of Truth will come into your consciousness from the Invisible—something that you did not consciously think of. In some moment of need, in some moment when a Word of Truth is necessary, in a moment when you are not consciously thinking Truth, God will put the word in your ear. This is the actual stage of spiritual consciousness when you begin to live by Grace.

When you can open your ear and receive impartations from within, when you receive the Word of God within you, that is when you are living by Grace. That is when you are taking no thought for your life, what you shall eat or what you shall drink, but are actually finding that there is an Invisible Presence bringing harmony into your experience without conscious human effort on your part. It is then that you know that there is an Invisible Presence, and this is when you come into the fuller attainment of spiritual consciousness.

There was a time when I was not aware of this indwelling Presence. Like Saul of Tarsus, I knew myself only as Joel Goldsmith, a businessman. I did not know that there was anything other than that until a particular day when I also "beheld the light." Thereafter I knew that the Spirit of God dwells in me and goes before me. The Spirit of God is the light unto my countenance. The Spirit of God is a lamp unto my feet. The Spirit of God is my high tower. It is my abiding place or my hiding place. It is my bread and my meat and my wine and my water. It is this Spirit of God that provides for me the words that I speak, the message that I write, the funds that carry it around the world, and the publishers who publish it. All of this is provided by the Spirit of God that dwelleth in me and that made Itself known to me in the moment of my attaining some measure of spiritual consciousness.

God is no respecter of persons; therefore you can be assured that there is a Spirit of God that dwells in you, call it what you will—the Christ, the Son of God, the Indwelling Spirit, the Messiah. *It* is invisible; *It* is incorporeal. You cannot see *It* or feel *It*; but you can experience *It* and know *It* by *Its* fruitage because with the realization of *Its* presence, you instantly lose all fear. No longer can you fear life or any of life's experiences, nor can you fear death. You come to the realization of Paul's revelation: "Neither life nor death can separate me from the love of God, the life of God, the will of God. Whatever the will of God is for me—on earth or on the next plane—be assured that the will of God will be done, because He planted His Son in me to see that it happens." This is true of you as well. If it were ever true of one individual and not of all others, there would be no true God. But there is one God, the one Father, and this Father is yours and mine. If this Father provided His Son to be born in me, He has provided His Son to be born in you— in proportion to your ability to open your consciousness to *It*, to surrender yourself to *It*, to be willing to live not by might nor by power, to put up your sword, to stop being angry, to stop being resentful, hateful, fearful. You cannot do it humanly, but the Grace of God makes it natural for all of these to disappear from your consciousness.

Open yourself to the Truth that the Spirit of God

dwells in you, closer to you than breathing, nearer than hands and feet. Above all, stop believing the theological nonsense that God deserts you in your moments of sin. It is in those very moments that you need God most, and do not believe that God could desert His own.

In any moment that you open your consciousness to the realization that a Son of God dwells in you, you will find the Master pointing His finger at you and saying, as He did to the woman taken in adultery, "Neither do I condemn thee. Thy sins be forgiven thee." You will hear Him saying, as He said to the thief on the cross, "I will take you with me into paradise this very night." In any moment that you open your consciousness to the realization that there is a Son of God, He will appear to you— not necessarily in form, but in consciousness—and you will hear or sense, "I am forgiven. I am free."

Principle of Prayer

The Infinite Way principle of prayer is that true prayer does not attempt to influence, manipulate, or use God. True prayer is not a prayer of petition because, as Scripture tells us, we do not know how to pray or what to pray for; we do not know how to go out or how to come in. We do not know what to pray for because we have no idea what our good tomorrow may be; it may have no relationship at all to today. Trying to continue our lives today as they were yesterday is what causes our discords.

It is difficult to give up our old habits when praying. However, the day comes when we are so desperate that we say, "Father, I don't know how to pray. You will have to take over." Before that day comes, learn to let God pray in you.

Attaining this attitude is difficult, but the way itself is simple. Simply agree that you have no desires. "I do not know what I want; I do not know what I need; I do not know anything about today or tomorrow; I am perfectly satisfied to wait, Father, for You to reveal Yourself. Thy will be done, not mine." As you wait in this attitude, you develop the ability to attain a state of receptivity in which God prays, God meditates, God communes in you.

Constant Conscious Abiding in Truth

The Infinite Way student cannot go through the day merely reading some Truth in the morning or anticipating hearing some Truth in the afternoon. There has to be a conscious activity of Truth going on all the time. That does not mean neglecting our human lives, duties, and activities. It means that we train ourselves to have some area of consciousness always active in Truth. Whether we look at the passing nature—trees, flowers, oceans—or whether we are constantly meeting people, we are active in our consciousness in finding some measure of God in the scene. In some way we have to train ourselves to behold the Presence and activity of God around us and to abide in the scriptural truths.

Proper Use of Scriptural Passages

Contemplating a scriptural passage for the purpose of accomplishing something is an improper use of Scripture. For example, to declare and repeat, "He performeth that which is given me to do," hoping to make it come true or to bring it about, is improper use. But when you have a task to do, occasionally remember that passage, then let the weight of the task drop off your shoulders and say with a smile, "Thank heaven there is a He." This is the proper use of that quotation. In other words, reminding ourselves of that which *is*, without trying through the use of an affirmation to *make* it so, is a proper use of a scriptural passage.

I am often told that I contradict myself by saying that we should not use an affirmation and then later using one. An affirmation as an affirmation is worthless, but an affirmation of Truth as a *reminder* that it *is* true is spiritual wisdom. Saying, "Thy Grace is my sufficiency in all things," and expecting that statement to *do* something for you is a mistake even if you recite it fifteen thousand times a day. That is a form of self-hypnosis. But occasionally repeating it within yourself as a reminder and saying, "Thank you, Father, for that reminder," and then letting the weight drop off your shoulders is a correct use.

In the fifteenth chapter of John we are told, "You are the branch, and Christ is the vine." We are reminded that if we live in that Truth and abide in that Word, we will bear fruit richly. That is, we will live harmonious, spiritual lives. But if we forget to live in that Word, if we do not abide in it and do not let it abide in us, we become as branches that are cut off, and we wither. Remembering the essence of the fifteenth chapter of John is a correct use of Scripture because once we know it and remember it, it is almost impossible to forget that "I and the Father are one," and we can then go about our day's work and let the day take care of itself.

We should all know such scriptural passages as the eighth chapter of Romans and realize that *only if* the Spirit of God dwells in us are we the children of God. If the

Spirit of God is not dwelling in us, we are mere mortals; and *mortal* means "of death." We are men and women of death if the Spirit of God does not dwell in us. How do we know if the Spirit of God is dwelling in us? If we are opening ourselves to the Spirit of God, then *It* is dwelling in us. If we are ignoring or neglecting *It*, then *It* is not dwelling in us. It is like saying that the Spirit of the Lord is everywhere, but the Spirit of the Lord is only where it is realized. The Spirit of the Lord potentially dwells in everybody, but *It* must be realized before *It* is an actuality.

CHAPTER 4

OVERCOMING OUR SENSE
OF SEPARATION FROM GOD

One of the principles of The Infinite Way is that the secret of harmonious, joyous, spiritual life is knowing God aright. Every individual has the right to be God-taught, God-inspired, God-supplied, God-healed, God-sustained, and God-maintained. However, you cannot turn to the Kingdom of God within and find God-realization while you entertain erroneous concepts of God, because these false concepts create a sense of separation from your own good. In order to make your contact with the Kingdom of God within and draw your good from it, you must understand the meaning of the word *God* and know the nature of God. You must know God aright. Do not accept the erroneous concepts you have been taught. They have been proven erroneous by their fruitage.

Erroneous Concepts of God

In the many centuries that have passed since human beings first experienced a sense of separation from God, we have sought something greater than ourselves that would meet our needs. Back in what we now call pagan days, the human race had many gods in accord with what humans wanted the god to do. They prayed to one god for beauty, to another for good weather, to another for fertility, and so forth. These pagan gods were looked upon to supply human needs: larger crops, larger herds, larger catches of fish, more rain, less rain, happiness, peace, and so on. The pagans even sacrificed animals, and sometimes humans, to these gods, hoping that the gods would fulfill their needs.

Asceticism evolved in which people fasted, gave away their possessions, did anything and everything possible to placate their gods, who were not performing according to what was expected of them.

Then we come to the Hebrew concept of one God. But you will notice that the Hebrews looked to that one God for the very same things that the pagans expected from their many gods. They approached God in the same ways. They sacrificed, they tithed, they tried to be good humans. Again, this was a paganistic concept of God, and their God was two-sided. He was a punishing God, and He was a rewarding God. If they were good, God rewarded them. If they did evil, God punished them. If they broke the laws, God punished them. They feared God's punishment. Fear of God became the dominant theme—not love of God, but fear of God. The Hebrew concept of God as a rewarding God or a punishing God was as erroneous as the pagan concepts of their gods.

God Neither Punishes Nor Rewards

You will not find a God of punishment or a God of reward in the teachings of the Master, Jesus Christ. He taught, "As ye sow, so shall ye reap," but He did not say that God would reward you if you were good or that God would punish you if you were evil. He made it very clear that the bread you cast on the water is what is returned to you. (If you express love, love comes back to you. If you express hate, hate comes back to you.) That does not say that God will punish you with lack if you do not cast bread on the water nor that He will reward you with abundance if you do. God does not punish bad behavior; God does not reward good behavior. That is the superparent concept of God.

God Does Not Withhold

"All that the Father hath is yours." It is not the nature of God to withhold from you and then give you those very things because you pray for them or because you have been good. That is the Santa Claus concept of God. As long as you entertain such a concept of God, you will lose your demonstration of supply; as long as you worship that type of God, you have no hope whatsoever of knowing God aright.

The more you realize that God is not a rewarding God or a punishing God, but that the nature of God is Infinite Love and Infinite Wisdom, the clearer you will see that there is no need to tell God of your needs or to ask Him to fulfill them. Doing so is going back to the pagan belief that God has been withholding from you. It is not in His consciousness to withhold anything from you or to punish you for anything.

The Nature of God

One of the first principles that an Infinite Way student must learn is the nature of God, and you cannot learn it by merely reading about it or hearing about it. However, by cogitating, pondering, or meditating on the message that you listen to or read, you can learn the nature of God from within your own being. The words or the message is the truth about Truth, but Truth reveals itself to you from within. The message must be taken into your consciousness and nurtured until, like a seed, it develops into a spiritual crop you can reap.

God is the power that maintains and sustains the universe. God is the creative principle, the law unto Its creation. By opening yourself to It, you will find It operating in your consciousness as a law of fulfillment. "I am come that ye might have life and that ye might have it more abundantly." This power has come, and it is available to all. It has not come so that you or I may have it and someone else not have it. God (or Spirit or Soul) refuses to work for only the Hebrew or for only the Protestant or for only the Catholic or for only saints. It functions equally for saints and sinners, for people of any religion, or for people of no religion. It functions for any color, race, or creed. It is a universal God. It is as free as air to each and every one, and just as available. But It cannot be brought into our experience for our exclusive use or to fulfill our individual needs or requirements.

God Does Not Hold Us in Bondage

Even the smallest measure of understanding of the nature of God would heal half of the diseases and discords of the world, because about half of the people of the world believe that God is punishing them for their sins. It is a theological belief that we are being punished for our sins—either of commission or omission—for which God is holding us in bondage. Anyone holding such beliefs has not even the faintest concept of the nature of God.

God is Spirit. God is Love. God is Infinite. God is Universal. Can an Infinite, Universal Love withhold itself? No more so than the law of gravity! If you drop an object, the law of gravity operates regardless of the value of the object. The law of gravity is no respecter of value. It operates for all. So it is with the Grace of God. It has no more power to discriminate saint from sinner than the law of gravity can discriminate a one-dollar object from a thousand-dollar object.

However, one cannot violate the law of God without producing discords—not because God withholds His Grace or because He is punishing the sinner, but because by violating the law of God *we* withhold ourselves from Grace. "Though your sins be scarlet, you are white as snow." The Master said to the thief on the cross, "I will take you into Paradise with me tonight." That was not a very long punishment for the crime, was it? Mary Magdalene's sins were forgiven as soon as she repented and indicated that her sins were behind her. Throughout the New Testament you will not find that Jesus ever held anyone in bondage for sinning. "Neither do I condemn thee. Go and sin no more lest a worse thing come upon you." Worse things befall you, not through God's punishing you, but because you reap what you sow.

If you condemn yourself for a past fault—a sin of omission or commission—and believe that you are being punished for it, realize that the nature of God is Love and Forgiveness. God's memory of your sins is short. You are the only one bringing your past offenses to your consciousness. You cannot live yesterday. There are no yesterdays in your experience except the yesterdays you carry over in your memory. God is not doing it. You are.

God Cannot Be Deceived

Always remember that the Spirit is closer to you than breathing. You can't deceive It because It is your self, It is your intelligence, It is your wisdom, It is the very guiding instinct of your being. Therefore, you cannot steal something and think God will not see you. God is right at the center of your being, and the moment you violate a spiritual principle, you are out of tune with It.

Acknowledge the Presence of God

Many people near death or suffering from disease believe that in some way they have become separated from God. Then they struggle and strive to find God. That is all wrong!

Regardless of appearances you have not become separated from God. Horrible sins and diseases, even roaring lions leaping on us, snipers shooting us down, or atomic bombs falling from the sky are only appearances that tempt us to believe that we have become separated from God. We become victims of that belief, because entertaining a sense of separation from God can be as disastrous and devastating as actual separation. In other words, the moment you accept the sense of separation from God, it is as if you had no God. So the thing to overcome is the sense of separation and not an actual separation.

There is only one way to overcome a sense of separation from God, and that is to acknowledge the activity and presence of God where you are. No other way has ever been discovered.

We hear and speak and write a great deal about searching for God, seeking God, trying to become one with God, making efforts to contact God. Every bit of that is wrong! I wish I could rewrite every passage in The Infinite Way writings that refers to seeking or searching for God or trying to make contact with God. In my earlier writings I was using the language of Scripture and of the religious world instead of writing what I knew in my heart.

Nothing we can do or think will enable us to find God. No effort will be successful! There is no need to search for God, because the Kingdom of God is within us. There has never been any need to search even before the days of Jesus Christ, because *the Kingdom of God is within you* had been said in different words thousands of years before the Master appeared on earth.

If the Kingdom of God is within us, where are we to search? What effort is necessary to find that which is within us? By the very act of seeking and searching for God, we are denying that the Kingdom of God is within us even though we know it and even voice it. The more we use physical or mental efforts to find God, the more we are denying that His Kingdom is within us!

Our relationship with God is, "I and the Father are one." One—not two! God is; therefore, I am. That is oneness. Every effort to make contact with God would be like Joel trying to make contact with Joel! Searching for God is searching for what is closer to us that breathing, nearer than our hands and feet! We are no farther from

God than we are from our own breathing, from our very being.

Praying, meditating, reading spiritual writings, attending services or classes or lectures are all a search for God; and the term *seeking God* can correctly be applied to these activities. But they are not the same as mentally or physically trying to make contact with God, which, if anything, tends to separate us from God, from the realization that God is within us.

"I Am Home in Thee"

It was a wonderful day in 1937 when the realization "I am home in Thee" came to me. I have related this experience in the chapter entitled, "Oh, Jerusalem, I Am Home in Thee" in my book *The Infinite Way*. Before this realization came to me, I was a weary wanderer in search of God, searching everywhere including the shelves of metaphysical libraries. All that time God was in me, and I was in God. I do not regret the years spent searching, because in the end the writings revealed what had always been true: I had never been away from "home." I just had not realized it. So let us neither tear up the books on Truth nor tear down the libraries, but let us bless every activity and means that help to reveal the Truth to us!

Once we have studied Scripture and inspirational writings, if we relax our mental efforts and are still enough, a whole new world opens to us: God reveals Itself to us. It is not necessary to be physically still. You can continue with your work or ride horseback or do housework or conduct business—anything at all as long as you are mentally still and open your inner ear and maintain a listening attitude. Then it can be revealed to you how close God is and why the poet could say so beautifully, "Closer than breathing, nearer than hands and feet." By being mentally still instead of seeking, searching, mentalizing, we can hear all that God has to say. Be sure that God has infinitely more interesting things to say to us than we could ever say to God!

Today would be a great day to give up our search for God and let God find us right where we are.

> Yea, though I make my bed in hell, God will find me there. If I walk through the valley of the shadow of death, God will find me there.

We do not have to search for or seek God. We only have to know that He is with us always and will never leave us or forsake us, and we can rest in that Word. When we do not, it is as if we pulled down our window shades and then went searching for sunlight!

The Kingdom of God is within you. Why search anymore? Simply acknowledge that God is closer than breathing, nearer than hands and feet. Acknowledge, "I and the Father are one, right here and now, and the place whereon I stand is holy ground. It makes no difference if where I am standing is hell." Remember that at some time and some place in our experience, each of us stands in hell. It may be the hell of sin; it may be the hell of disease; it may be the hell of lack and limitation, of unemployment, of danger, of insecurity. All of these things are hellish, horrid experiences, but they become transformed when we realize that even in the midst of this hell, "Thou art here. I do not have to search for God even in this hell, for Thou art here even though I walk through the valley of the shadow of death." Acknowledge, "The place whereon I stand is holy ground." Why? Because God is there. Why search for God, who is standing in your shoes?

Since God is omnipresent, can God be away from where you are? Since God fills all space and time, is there some place or time away from where God can be? The Father is in the midst of you, wherever you are. He is omnipresent, always present.

Demonstrate Omnipresence

Practice the conscious awareness of Omnipresence until you achieve a complete consciousness of Omnipresence. Instead of searching for God, acknowledge:

> The Father is in the midst of me, not where I am seeking and searching, but within me. When? Now, when I acknowledge Him, because He is omnipresent, always present. Thank you, Father, Thou art here! I shall not fear what mortals can do to me. I shall not fear any presence or power in heaven, on earth, or in hell, for Omnipresence is with me. The Presence of God goes with me and before me to make the crooked places straight. The Presence remains behind me to bless all those who pass that way. The Presence walks on each side of me.

Fulfill yourself with the realization of Omnipresence as the first point to practice before going on to the next one.

God Is All-Inclusive

By demonstrating Omnipresence, we find all things automatically included. Scriptural language says that all things are "added unto us," but in the Infinity of God, all things are already included. Being all things, God includes health, supply, home, companionship, opportunity, transportation, talent, ability, genius, and so on. Therefore, there is only one demonstration to make: the demonstration of God's Presence, the realization of Omnipresence.

Thinking of supply, companionship, or home as things separate and apart from God and then trying to demonstrate them actually separates us from these things.

God is the only health there is and the only supply there is. There is no peace, no satisfaction, no safety, no security except in and through God. No happy people live on earth except those who have found a measure of God. Young people may find temporary satisfaction in physical health, in outer companionship, and joy in the handling of money, but those are temporary. I am sure there come to them moments of void, moments of blankness, when they wonder what it is all about. Aside from the very young who are still delighting in the joys of the outer world, it is safe to say that no men or women on earth have ever found happiness or achieved peace of mind or soul except to the degree that they have realized God.

Many have found wealth without God, but many also have found that it was not a permanent dispensation and have lost their wealth in one way or another. Many have found health, but eventually something comes along to deprive them of it. I know millionaires who have everything in the world but God, and they are very busy seeking the one thing they do not have and neglecting all they do have. I know many people in perfect physical and mental health who in other ways are in utter agony. But by realizing God, there is no way you can lose health, wealth, home, or companionship, because God *is* our health, harmony, home, joy, and peace of mind. God does not send it to us or give it to us; God simply *is*. Once we understand that God is the fullness of being, the only demonstration we have to make is the demonstration of *I*.

When we have the *I*, all things are added unto us and abundance is made manifest. "*I* am come that ye might have life and have it more abundantly." Ask yourself, "What good would health be if I did not have God? What good would supply be, or a home or companionship, if I did not have God?"

Your Living Is Provided by Grace

The human concept of supply is that we obtain our living through our work and labor and by being worthy of it. False teaching has brought us to the human belief that we obtain a living through our labors. Our living has nothing to do with our work; our living is provided by Grace.

It was never intended that we should labor mentally or physically for supply. A child does not work for its living, yet it gets a very good one. All meals, clothing, housing, education, and even vacations are provided for a child without its lifting a finger for them or even thinking about them. In the same way, God provides for all His children. It would be a strange Father indeed if He did not provide for His offspring! It is the Father's good pleasure to give you His Kingdom. Therefore, the spiritual concept of supply is Omnipresence.

Of course, we have our occupations or professions, but we should engage in them for the joy of working. We perform what is given us to do and we do it for the sake of doing it well, not for the sake of earning a living. You will find that sometimes you derive less income from your occupation or profession than from the many other sources of income or supply that open up.

In other words, you should derive as much joy in your occupation or profession as I get from my work. Certainly,

I would not engage in this work to earn a living. I would be very glad to do it if there were no income from it! As a matter of fact, when you are called to this work, you find that you would gladly sacrifice all the living in the world just for the joy of being in this work. And so it should be with any art, profession, occupation, or job that you may be called to do. It should be your joy to do it.

When we give up the human, mental concept of making a living or earning a living or working for a living and realize that our work is merely what is given us to do today, two things happen. Our work may not be the kind that we enjoy to the fullest, but if we accept it and give it the best we can at each moment, gradually we are lifted out of it and into what to us represents a higher or more noble form of work. The second thing is that happens is that when we give up our human concept of earning a living, we find that our living is provided to us by Grace. It is forever pouring itself through to us. It may come in the mail or in our paychecks or from our investments. All we have to do is wake up and accept it.

We are so used to the idea of laboring and being worthy of our good that at first it is a greater struggle for us to accept it than it is to labor for it. But now is the time to develop the ability to relax and let our living come to us by Grace. You may think, "Why, this is impossible! All I get is what I earn or what my husband earns or what I inherited." That is not true at all in the spiritual kingdom, which is right here and now when we give up our human concepts of supply.

The greatest lesson The Infinite Way has to offer is the often-repeated Truth that we need seek and find only God and leave everything else alone. "Seek ye first the Kingdom of God," and the rest of these things will be added unto us. (The words *seek* and *find* are used in the sense that praying, meditating, reading spiritual writings, attending services or classes or lectures are a searching for God.)

Realize Omnipresence

Let us give up all attempts to demonstrate employment, income, companionship, home, health, wealth, freedom, joy, peace of mind, even sinlessness. Let us give up even the desire to be good and pure. Cleanse the temple, clean the house of all the old desires until our only desire is to realize God's Presence, to realize Omnipresence, to get acquainted with God and know Him aright.

It is difficult at first to know God aright because we think of Him in terms of our concepts of God. It may be Jesus' concept of God as Father or as the Father within. Or it may be Paul's concept of God as the Christ. It may be your own concept or your parents' concept or your church's concept, or it may be the metaphysical concept of God as Mind, Life, or Principle. All these concepts are only facets of God. Love is only one of the many ways in which God presents Himself. Mind is only one of the many ways in which God presents Himself. Law is only one of the many ways in which God presents Himself.

So let us give up the kind of God that we have been taught or visualized or believed in. Instead of thinking of God in some finite, limited way, let us realize that Life, Truth, Love, Substance, Principle, Law, Soul, Spirit are all ways in which God presents Itself to us, but that God is even greater than the sum total of all these facets. Let us not be concerned with what we have been taught about God or what our books say that God is, and let us go for the whole vision. Let us turn with an open mind to the revelation of God, the unfolding of God, in our consciousness and be prepared for It in whatever form It may appear. To each one the revelation will come in a different way.

Those who have experienced God cannot tell you what the experience is like, but they will tell you that God is not like anything they expected. I could tell you some of the ways in which I have caught glimpses of God, but my account would be incomplete and imperfect because I have no way of explaining Allness. Allness will appear to you in one way one day and in another way another day.

Each one of us will experience God in a different way, and trying to describe it would be like the three blind men describing an elephant to the others. One felt the elephant's tail and told the others that the elephant was a heavy rope. Another felt the elephant's leg and said that the elephant was a tree so wide that one could not reach around it with both arms and so heavy that one could not move it. The other felt a tusk and said, "Why, no! An elephant is not like that at all. It is cold and hard." Each blind man described the elephant from his own perspective. But the elephant was actually more than the sum total of all those things.

So let us give up our old concepts of God and turn to the revelation of God Itself. "Acquaint now thyself with God and be at peace." You know that being at peace, you will have health, wealth, harmony, and all the other things too, or you would not be at peace. To get peace, get acquainted with God, and all these things will be added.

Let us give up the desire for anything or anybody on the outer plane until our hearts can say, "My soul longeth. . . . My heart and my flesh crieth out for the living God."[1] "My soul thirsteth for God, for the living God."[2] "My heart panteth."[3] The God-hungry person says, "Give me God! The whole world is well worth losing as long as I have God, only God!"

When Jesus said, "I have overcome the world," He did not mean, "I have demonstrated the world or won the world or got the world." No, He had overcome all desires and needs because He had found God; and, in finding His God, He found all things necessary to His fulfillment. Even though He had no mother, father, sister, brother, or friends, He was well satisfied without them because He was completely filled with God. He was not happy with kings, emperors, princes, or even the religious leaders. His only companionship was in those who were of His household, of His own consciousness.

Of course, the things that filled Jesus may not completely meet our needs. God may fulfill Itself in our experience as companionship on the level of friends, relatives, family, husband, wife, or fellow students. I am sure, though, that the day would come, in this experience or another, when we also would feel, "No, none of these means anything to me. Those who are spiritually one with me constitute my fulfillment."

In time, all of us will come to that place where we will have little interest in anybody in the outer world who is not of our spiritual household regardless of their blood relationship. Then our companionship will be with each other. Our fulfillment will be with God in, through, and with each other.

---

[1] Psalm 84:2.
[2] Psalm 42:2.
[3] Psalm 38:10.

Give up all desire for home, companionship, money, or supply in any form. Let your only desire be to realize God's presence, realize Omnipresence, to realize, "I and the Father are one, and all that the Father hath is mine." Having made that demonstration, is there any need to demonstrate anything else? The only demonstration to make is the realization of the Truth.

Keep your thoughts stayed on God. Learn to meditate. Be quiet! Be still! Let God touch you with His finger! Let God reveal Himself to you; and God revealing and manifesting Himself will appear in outer form as the things necessary to your daily living.

CHAPTER 5

THE FRUITAGE OF KNOWING
GOD ARIGHT

To know God aright, you must first of all know that God is in the midst of you—not separate and apart from you. If you think God is external to yourself, you do not know God aright. God is not to be gained or won or searched for. God is to be recognized as one's Self (Self is capitalized to indicate the Infinite Self individualized as your self and mine). God is really your Self, the *I* that is really God-being, the Son of God, the Christ of God; God individualized, God in individual expression. When you know this, you do not look outside yourself; instead, you inwardly relax with the thought, "God *is* closer to me than breathing. I do not have to go *to* God for anything because God knows my need before I do." It is not God in heaven who knows your needs; it is God in the midst of you that knows, and "it is His good pleasure to give you the Kingdom."

You do not earn God's Grace; nor can you deserve it. Nobody could humanly be good enough to deserve God's Grace; but it is ours by right of inheritance. The *I* of our being is the Child of God, and it is joint heir with Christ to all of the heavenly riches. Whether we earn it or deserve it or not has nothing to do with the fact that as the Child of God you cannot be disinherited.

The Nature of God As Fulfillment

God is fulfillment. God is fulfilling *Itself*. If you need a material symbol, think about the sun. The sun is shining and pouring fourth its warmth and light. In other words, the sun is fulfilling itself as the sun. You would not pray to the sun to give *more* light or *more* warmth. If you were to pray, your prayer would be an inner realization of *is*. The sun *is* shining; the sun *is* warm; the sun *is* light. You know that whatever the sun is, it *is*, and it is about its business and fulfilling itself as warmth and light.

God Is the Creator

God is the creative principle. The Father in Heaven is the only parent. If you believe that you benefit or suffer in accord with whether your earthly parents are rich or poor, good or bad, generous or not generous, you are not living spiritually. God, the Father, is the maintaining and sustaining principle. He is the only source of your good. We can respect our human parents and be as affectionate as we want to on the human level, but acknowledge that God is our only Father, the Creator, who maintains and sustains us.

Unless you have the strong conviction that your Heavenly Father within you already knows your needs and it is His good pleasure to give you the Kingdom, you cannot live spiritually on the subject of supply. You will always be looking to "man whose breath is in his nostrils." You will look to a parent or a wife or a husband or a child. When all these fail, you will turn to the government and ask them for your pittance. Why? Because you have chosen to live by the human belief that your good comes to you through human good. Live in the realization that there is a He within you and that it is His good pleasure to give you the Kingdom and He knows your needs before you do.

God, the Only Love

There are many forms of love: marital love, parental love, filial love, brotherly and sisterly love, neighborly love, and community love. Love is a major factor in our existence. We are made happy by and through love, and we are made miserable by its absence. Why should there be an absence? There is no actual absence of love. We only experience an absence of love because of our ignorance. In our human existence we look to each other for love, for cooperation, for friendship. Therein do we make our mistake. If we look to each other, we may find love today and hate tomorrow. We may find gratitude today and ingratitude tomorrow. We may find cooperation today and a lack of it tomorrow.

We should look only to God for love. God is Love, and God is the activity of love. Since God is Infinite and Universal, when we find our love in God, we find it in each other. If we will realize that all love is an emanation of God, we will then find love in those whom we meet on this path. The few who do not respond to this will drop out of our experience, and our world will be made up of those who do love us on the plane of consciousness in the way of love natural to the relationship.

In the moment we are enfolded in His love, His love permeates our being. His love is the central theme of our being. His love is our life, and the nature of love is forgiveness. Who loves and holds in condemnation? Who loves and holds a memory of something to be forgiven? In the heart of the lover there is no condemnation; there is compassion. There is no condemnation from parent to child, no condemnation from lover to beloved. There is no condemnation wherever there is love. We do not hold those we love in condemnation.

God's love is all-inclusive and takes under its wing all of being, your being and mine, saint and sinner alike. Until you understand that this is the nature of God, you cannot know Him aright.

On one wall of every Christian Science church is a sign that states, "Divine Love always has met and always will meet every human need." As I sat in a Christian Science church one evening, I looked around at all the people I knew there and thought, "It isn't so! I know too many who have waited years for that Divine Love to meet their needs, and it just has not happened." Then I pondered on Mrs. Eddy's reasons for choosing those words, because she must have had a special reason. As I pondered, it suddenly dawned on me that Mrs. Eddy was right but that the people had not interpreted the words correctly. Divine Love is not something in outer space; Divine Love is inside. Therefore, it is the Divine Love that we express that meets our human needs. Unless we are expressing an impersonal, impartial, universal love, there is no love meeting our needs. That evening I saw that there is no Divine Love out there somewhere; God is not out there somewhere meeting our needs. God and His Divine Love are within us; but as long as we are not expressing it, it cannot meet our human needs.

Divine Love constitutes forgiveness, charity, benevolence, kindness, cooperation, sharing. All of these, and any others you can possibly think of, constitute Divine Love. If we do not express Divine Love, it will not be returned to us to meet our needs. As you can imagine, this realization brought a change into my way of life, because I saw then how foolish it is to sit around waiting for God to do something. That would make God a do-nothing, and that cannot be because God is forever being God.

God Is the Only Power

Of course, we believe that we do accept God as the only Power and that we are obedient to the first commandment, but the truth is that none of us is entirely obedient to that commandment; and the fruitage comes only in the proportion that we obey.

How are we to obey the first commandment? By establishing within ourselves from earliest morning that we will not recognize any other power but God's. We will acknowledge God as the only power operating in our consciousness or in the consciousness of those with whom we will come in contact. We begin our day with the realization that no man, woman, or child can give to us or withhold from us since God is the only source and activity of our good, and God is the only power.

Every day you face fears that are common in the world. You may fear that your banker will refuse you a loan or your customer will not buy from you or some individual in someway has the power to withhold something from you. When you indulge in such fears, you are placing power in "man whose breath is in his nostrils." Yet we are told, "Wherein is he to be accounted of?"

As long as we even mildly entertain the belief that good can be given to us or withheld from us by someone, we are not obeying the first commandment and we are preventing ourselves from receiving our good. Let me illustrate that.

God, the Only Source of Truth

You may believe that Truth can come to you from me. That is not so, because God is the Source and Activity of all Truth, and I am here for the same purpose as you are: to receive Truth from God. I have no Truth to give and none to withhold. I only hold myself in conscious union with God so that Truth can flow through me from the Godhead to whomever is receptive and responsive. At this moment my body, mouth, tongue, or mind is being used as the instrument through which Truth is reaching us from God. I have no power to give or withhold Truth. If we realize that we are gathered together to receive Truth only from God, all of us will receive some measure of God-Truth. But if either you or I believe that I have Truth to give you, the Truth may very well be blocked from us.

God, the Only Supply

Some of you remember the Great Depression, when many experienced a lack of supply. There was no lack or shortage! The land was full of cattle; the air was full of birds; the oceans were full of fish. Where was the lack? If anything, there was an oversupply. There was such an abundance that great quantities were thrown into the ocean or burned or plowed under or stored in warehouses, as as they have been since then. There is no lack of supply!

God is Supply! When we have God, we have supply. Our task is to acknowledge God and realize Him as the Activity, the Source, and the Law of supply. We must acknowledge God as our sufficiency—not look to our jobs, our money, our rich relatives, benevolences, or government. Like Moses, we may find manna falling from the sky, if it cannot come any other way, or water from the rocks. Or, like Elijah, we may find cakes baked on the very stones in front of us or ravens bringing food or a widow sharing her mite.

Anything can happen, and be assured there will be an abundance. Abundance can be experienced by each and every one of us the moment we no longer rely on "man whose breath is in his nostrils" and realize God as the Source.

If you hold in your consciousness that God is the only Source of your supply, you will always have your supply made evident to you even before you need it, regardless of what anyone does. The blockage is only in your belief that someone can give it or withhold it. For example, there is no better way for a salesperson to fail than to believe that business depends upon the goodwill of customers. That is a fine way to limit one's self! Understanding God as the activity of all business may not compel Jones or Smith to buy from you, but it will result in an abundance of sales every week, many times not from the customers you expect. What difference does it make to whom you make the sales? The important thing is that the sales be made!

You may say, "But I *do* recognize God as the Source!" How often and how consistently do you? It must be more than an occasional thought. It must be a continuous activity until your consciousness is so imbued with the realization of God as the Source that it becomes automatic and you no longer need to consciously think of it. Then the flow begins.

God, the Only Life

We have accepted that you have a life and I have a life and a newborn baby has a life. That is not true! We do have a life, but it is not a life of our own. The only life we have is God. If there is only one God and He is Life, there can be only one life, and that is God's. Then how can there be young life, old life, diseased life, weak life, or dying life? As we obey the first commandment and acknowledge that there is only one God and as we become imbued with God as the One Life, every appearance of disease, age, and death begins to fade and we become aware of the one, harmonious, perfect Life expressed as your individual being and mine. We become aware of the vital, spiritual life within us at all times and at all ages.

God, the Law and the Substance

Acknowledge God as the only Power, the only Source, and the only Law. This acknowledgment immediately begins to nullify every belief in the laws of heredity, of food, of climate, of infection, and of contagion—all material law. In the proportion that you accept God as the One Law and the only Law, material law is nullified. Every time laws of economics, politics, physics, or jurisprudence come to your attention, think back to, "Thank you, Father. I know there is only one Law and that is the law of God because there is only one God and there can be but one law and, since God is Spirit, law must be spiritual."

We are continually meeting bodily conditions that testify to growth or lack of bodily substance. God is the only Substance, and there cannot be an overabundance or an insufficiency of God. By acknowledging God as the Divine Substance, you will soon find that the body is showing forth the normalcy of God.

God, the Harmony in All Things

We are constantly presented with outer appearances of sin, disease, death, lack, and limitation, which we call pictures of error. But the pictures begin to change as our spiritual consciousness develops and unfolds and as we behold the Invisible as the source of harmony. The Invisible is the reality of all that exists. Therefore, we do not accept appearances at face value but let Truth remove the discordant appearances.

Rest in God

The fruitage of knowing God aright depends on your knowing, first of all, that God is your selfhood and the selfhood of everyone you meet. Second, it depends on your knowing that the Father within you knows your need so that you do not have to tell Him about it. Third, you must know that it is His good pleasure to give you the Kingdom. Then you just relax in that assurance. When you have that assurance, you are really living the spiritual life.

You must realize that this God upon whom you are relying is not external to you or separate and apart from you, but is your own selfhood under the name of I, the I that is at the center of your being, which you call your Self, the I that is the offspring of God, the God individualized as you, the Christ, Son of God, who is heir of God, and with whom you are joint heir to all of the heavenly riches.

As you abide in that word, do all the things you are given to do without thought of result or reward. Remember that God does not reward. Whatever God does, He does merely as a function of God. Remember the sun. The sun does not give light and warmth as a reward to anyone for anything. Warmth and light are the sun's function, and it cannot withhold them. So it is with God. God cannot withhold, not even from the sinner. God does not have such human qualities. He is not a human being. Therefore, God does not act like a human parent or a judge. God is Infinite Being and is forever *being*. God cannot give, and God cannot withhold. God can only *be*.

Knowing this truth brings that God-being into active experience in your life. You are called upon only to know the truth about God. Then you will relax in God.

Spiritual Wisdom

When you know the nature of God, when you no longer think you know better than God, when you no longer believe there is something you can tell God, when you no longer expect God to do something for one individual that He is not doing equally for everyone, when you no longer behold God as a power to be used to destroy your enemies—that is the beginning of spiritual wisdom, and you will experience the fruitage of knowing God aright.

Getting Spiritual Understanding

To know God aright is to experience harmony, life eternal, completeness, and perfection of being. If we are experiencing lack and limitation in any form—health, supply, human relationships, and so forth—we must acknowledge to ourselves that we do not know God aright. It is up to us to begin the study of God at whatever point we find ourselves. Some may find themselves believers in paganistic gods. Others may find themselves, as I did, with no religious background except the Ten Commandments. Others may find themselves in orthodox churches, others in metaphysical teachings or mental teachings. Wherever you find yourself, that is where you must begin to know God aright. There is no use in wishing for a better place to start. Start from where you happen to be, and advance from that point by whatever means are available to you.

Where shall you find the right understanding of God? You will find the right knowledge only within yourself. You will not find it in any book. The right books can be a tremendous help in getting you back into your Self where you will meet and know God aright. They are a source of inspiration and can lift you up out of yourself, but that is all they can do. They cannot reveal God to you. God is revealed only in one place—within you, because the Kingdom of God is within you.

I was twenty-one years of age before I even opened a Bible. At that point the realization came to me that there *is* a God. My search for God began at that point. It led me through many, many ways—some of them good and some of them misguided, to say the least. My search brought me to whatever unfoldment is now mine; and as you all know, my unfoldment is neither final nor complete.

On this spiritual path, we may find ourselves backsliding. After moving well along on the path and believing that we have found Him aright, we may later learn that we have found only a substitute and sometimes not even a very satisfactory one. In that case, we can go back and start over again, or we can take what little good we may have found and proceed from there. You may experience moments of discouragement, especially when you are not making the progress you expect, but those periods should be brief, not lasting more than a day at a time.

If we honestly acknowledge that any sense of discord in our experience is the result of our lack of understanding God, we will demonstrate our first achievement of the realization of God. Your entire search will be devoted to *knowing God aright*—not to demonstrating health, harmony, supply, a home, or companionship. There is much more to the spiritual life than merely demonstrating health, supply, and so forth.

A major step leading to the realization of God is pondering God, meditating on God, holding God as a reality within our being. God *is*. He is the central point of all existence, and there is no way to have life eternal except to know Him aright, to know God as *God is*—not the concepts of God that we have been taught, but God *Itself*.

CHAPTER 6

THE ARMOR OF ONENESS

The foundation of all Truth teachings—whether it is Christian Science, Unity, New Thought, or The Infinite Way—is that we live and move and have our being in God. All of them agree on that point.

Some orthodox traditions may teach that we *will* live in God at some future time, but Truth movements agree that *now* we are the children of God, *now* we are in the secret place of the Most High, *now* we live and move and have our being in God. But Truth teachings (whether organized or unorganized) cannot *make* us live as if we were living and moving and having our being in God; they can do something for us only in the proportion that we permit it.

I would like to tell you about a minister and his wife, both of them very serious Truth students, whom I met in London. In World War II during the German blitz of London, those who could were building bomb shelters in their gardens. But these two people had dedicated their

71

lives to the understanding that they lived in God and that their lives took place in the secret place of the Most High; therefore, how could any form of discord or inharmony come nigh their dwelling place? They decided to have nothing to do with bomb shelters, but to serve as fire wardens in their neighborhood during actual bombings.

Their neighborhood, situated between the largest London airport and a major railway, was constantly bombarded. Not a single night went by that their section of the city was not bombed. The airport and railway were often severely damaged and each time had to be repaired so that the railroad and air force could resume operations. The bomb shelter of one of their neighbors received a direct hit, and the whole family was wiped out. Throughout this entire time, the minister and his wife were never even scratched and not a window of their home was blown out!

To human sense, this was indeed one of the miracles of the war. But to this couple, it was the most natural thing in the world because they lived in God and therefore nothing could come nigh their dwelling place.

Truth teaching cannot make us accept this Truth so deeply that we can do without bomb shelters. No one can accept it for us; it is something that we must do individually. This teaching, this secret of life, is given to us—but we must individually accept it and then live it.

In God We Have Our Being

We have our being in God, because we are an emanation of God and we are therefore the Divine Consciousness Itself. It is only in the "insanity of our humanhood" that we have left our Father's house.

*Does the fish soar to find the ocean? Does the
eagle plunge to find the air? that we ask of the stars
in motion if they have rumors of Thee there?*[1]

Does the fish seek the ocean? No! The fish *is* in the
ocean. It may not know that it is in the ocean, but it
certainly knows that it is in its rightful place, and it goes
about its rightful business without any attempt to find the
ocean. But let us imagine that the fish in a moment of
insanity (supposing there is such a thing as fish insanity)
has lost its perception and is not aware that it is in the sea
and so starts swimming madly up and down searching for
the ocean! That *would* be insanity!

In our seeking and searching for God, we are suffering
from the same kind of insanity, because we have never left
our Father's house. When we search for the Presence and
the Power of God to dissolve our discords and inharmonies, we are in a state of humanhood as unnatural as the
fish seeking the ocean! As long as we seek for a God or a
Truth or a treatment or a prayer to relieve us of our
problems, just that long will our problems remain with us.
We will continue to be overwhelmed with the discords and
inharmonies of this world until we achieve this spiritual
discernment:

> I am already in the secret place of the Most High. I
> am living and moving and having my being in God,
> and I am about my Father's business.

Spiritual Discernment

Before illumination we see good people and bad ones, sick
ones and healthy ones, good powers and bad powers.

---

[1]From "The Kingdom of God," by Francis Thompson.

Seeing evil is merely our ignorance of what we are beholding. Let me illustrate this.

People ignorant of art may behold an oil painting done by a master and say that it is only daubs of paint on canvas. To them that is all it is and can ever be; they cannot appreciate it. Yet the person who has learned art appreciation goes into raptures over it. So it is with music. Some will hear a magnificently performed symphony and think that it sounds terrible, while others sitting beside them are in raptures. The difference is art appreciation and music appreciation. Through an appreciation of art or music, we behold what those without it can never know.

When we have been touched by the Spirit, we have "spiritual appreciation," which we call spiritual consciousness or spiritual awareness or spiritual discernment. With it, what has heretofore been unreal, ephemeral, and transcendental becomes the reality, the heart and soul of our experience, of our entire lives, and the things of the outer world become the shadows. Oh yes, we continue to eat and drink and sleep and enjoy, but the things of the outer world never move us or thrill us to the same extent as the things of the inner world that we now perceive. With spiritual consciousness,

> Oh world invisible, we view thee; Oh world intangible, we touch thee; Oh world unknowable, we know thee; Inapprehensible, we clutch thee.[2]

Who is this *we*? The world does not see the invisible, the world does not touch this intangible Presence, the world does not know the unknowable, and the world cannot clutch that invisible Divine Presence; so it is not the world. This *we* are those of spiritual perception, those

---

[2]The Kingdom of God.

who have turned to the Father within and have caught at least *some* realization of this inner Presence, this inner Light, this inner glow. It is only through this inner vision that it is possible to clutch, to hold on to, the realization that to the rest of the world is intangible and inapprehensible.

That is why Scripture tells us,

> Awake thou that sleepest, and arise from the dead, and Christ shall give thee light. [3]

What do you find when you awaken from the human dream? You will not find yourself floating around with a pair of wings! You will still be walking the same earth with the same feet. You will be looking out with the same eyes, but you will behold an entirely different scene. No longer will you see good people and bad people, sick people and well people, high people and low people.

At the moment of awakening, you will behold God alone as Infinite Being and as individual being, and you will realize your true identity. With this inner vision you will view "Thee, the world invisible, the Son of God invisible in man." With your inner vision you will now behold that there is only good—not good and evil.

Let us at least begin to view this invisible universe, this invisible Truth, in the realization that right now the fish is swimming in its waters, right now the eagle is flying through the air, and in the same degree right now "I live and move and have my being in God." With all of your imagination, you cannot visualize the fish being out of the water nor the eagle out of the air. If only you will take that picture into your mind, you will understand how and why you and I cannot get outside of God. We cannot get

---

[3]Ephesians 5:14.

outside the realm of God, nor can we get the realm of God outside our own being, because we live and move and have our being in God and the Kingdom of God is within us.

It is a paradox, but it is nevertheless true, that just as a drop of water is in the ocean, so the ocean is in a drop of water. Oh, physically that may not be possible, but spiritually you will find that it is true. Spiritually you will learn that you live and move and have your being in God, and God lives and moves and has *Its* being in you—because of Oneness. God is Infinite Being; God is the Infinite Consciousness. Therefore, since God is the only Being and the only Consciousness, God is our individual consciousness. "All that the Father is, I am," even though I may not at any given moment be able to demonstrate the Allness and the Fullness. That comes only by progressive unfoldment.

Today we may be a worm in the dust and feel unworthy to sit at His feet. With a little spiritual enlightenment we may come to the point where we say, "Oh, no! I am a Truth student and something higher than a worm in the dust." Then a little more enlightenment comes, and we say, "I am the child of God." That brings more enlightenment, and we say, "Not only am I the child of God, but I am heir, joint heir, with Christ to all the heavenly riches." We seem to be growing now, but we are not. We are merely becoming more and more aware of what we already are, always have been, and always will be. We have not changed from a worm in the dust to the very Christ of God. We have merely awakened from our human slumbers and realized, "I already am, I always have been." We then go on and assume our "new" identity and live in the world as though it were true—which it is, but we have not heretofore realized it.

You may be sure that for quite some time to come, we will be faced with temptations: temptation to believe that we are not living and moving and having our being in God; temptation to accept a sense of separation from God; temptation to accept sin, disease, death, lack, limitation as actual conditions that we must overcome. When these temptations come, the remedy is, "Thank you, Father, I am home in Thee. I am in the secret place of the Most High. In spite of this appearance, I will fear no evil, for I and the Father are one, and all that the Father hath is mine."

The more you make use of the words *is* and *am*, the more you realize that because the Lord *is* my Shepherd, I shall not want, the nearer you will come to the realization of your true being. Do not seek to find the Lord or make the Lord your Shepherd, do not search for the Shepherd; just realize that the Lord *is* your Shepherd, then face any appearance of lack or limitation in the safety and security of that Truth. Truth is our hiding place and our abiding place. When we abide in that Truth and let that Word abide in us, we have our remedy for every temptation.

We do not have to seek or search for remedies, for treatment, or for prayers because we already live and move and have our being in God. All we have to do is be still and realize, "Thank you, Father, it is done." In any situation, "Be not afraid. It is *I*. *I* am in the midst of you. *I* am with you. *I* will never leave you nor forsake you." But remember that we make it tangible in our experience only as we accept this in our consciousness. The fact that it is true will not help you. Only the conscious realization of this Truth will help you. This Truth applies to everybody, whether in hospitals, in prisons, in wars, or in poverty, but this Truth is not helping them or the world at large. Why?

Because of the insanity of the sense of separation from God that has been set up within us.

As long as you believe that you are somewhere outside of God and keep trying to get back in, or as long as you seek to bring God into your experience, you are continuing that sense of separation from God. The only way to overcome your sense of separation is to acknowledge here and now,

> Lean not unto thine own understanding. Acknowledge Him in all thy ways and He will give thee rest. Though I make my bed in hell, Thou art here. If I walk through the valley of the shadow of death, I will fear no evil, for Thou art here. That which I am seeking, I already am. God in the midst of me is mighty. The Lord *is* my Shepherd. I *am* in the secret place of the Most High. I am about my Father's business. All that the Father is, I am. My eyes are closed to discords and inharmonies and temptations. I do not see or hear evil.

Oh, yes, you will see them with your eyes and hear them with your ears, but you will not accept them as reality. You will see them as shadows with no reality and so you will neither fear them nor hate them nor love them nor give power to them. Never give power to appearances, because "Thou shalt have no other Gods"—no other Power. Yes, for a long time you will see error with your eyes and will hear error with your ears. You will smell it and taste it and touch it, but you will not give power to it. You need not walk around denying it or ignoring it. Simply look right at it, and then give it no power. Acknowledge God alone as Power. "Since the Kingdom of God is within me, All Power is within me."

Since All Power is within you, look at anything out in the world and realize that it can have no power. "How can the mind of any person out there have power when the Kingdom of God, the Kingdom of All Power is within me? How can a disease germ have power when the Kingdom of God is within me? How can anything or anybody or any circumstance or any condition have power when All Power is within me and is flowing from the within to the without?" Then you can look at any person, any place, any thing, any circumstance and say, "You could have no power over me unless it came from the Father in heaven." Christ Jesus could say it to Pilate, because He had acknowledged the Kingdom of God, the All-Power within.

Once you establish within your consciousness this great Truth, how can you ever love, hate, or fear something or someone? How can you give power to somebody's good thought or bad thoughts? Nobody's good thoughts can heal you; nobody's bad thoughts can harm you. No power out there can ever disturb you unless you yourself give it power. It is like fearing a shadow on the wall and running from it because it looks like a man, sometimes a big one! But it is only a shadow! If the Kingdom of God is within you, then All Power is within you and, like Paul, you can say, "None of these things and none of these people can harm me. Not even bombs can harm me. Nothing external to me can move me, since All Power is within." We do not use a Truth of this kind as a weapon over some evil power. We merely cling to this Truth and use it as a constant reminder of the Truth of being. Then soon that Truth takes over in our consciousness, and it then becomes a law unto our experience.

This Truth in our consciousness is our armor. But using the word *armor* sets up a sense of defense, and the moment we think in terms of defense, we are in trouble. What shall we be defended against if God is All-Being and All-Power? For that reason, in The Infinite Way we see God as the One Power, the Only Power, and so we use the term *the armor of Oneness.*

Putting On the Armor of Oneness

God as One is one of the greatest revelations in all spiritual teaching, yet it is only touched upon in the very highest spiritual teachings. It is not merely a statement of God as One; it is a revelation. God is One; the One and only Power and Presence; One Life that does not have to be saved; One Life that does not have to be healed; One Soul that does not have to be purified; One Substance; One Activity.

God being the only Substance, there is no bad substance, no evil substance, not too much substance, not too little substance. Therefore you do not need any words or thoughts or things with which to change substance.

God is the only Activity. Who can fear God's activity? Therefore you do not need any words or thoughts or armor of offense or defense. Oh, yes, we are tempted to believe in other activity! At the first street corner there may be a gunman to hold us up, and our first temptation is to use either physical might or mental power to overpower him. But spiritual Truth says, "Stand ye still. The battle is not yours." There is no Power but God; there is no Activity but God's. So let the gunman have his fun with his little gun if he wants!

When atomic bombs are falling, everybody wants to build a bomb shelter or a mental wall or mental defense. Against what? The activity of God? There is no other activity! In a Christian world whose whole teaching is based on God as the only Activity, why should one be fearful? Bombs can only be another temptation, like germs.

We of the metaphysical world are not nearly as afraid of germs as the rest of the world, so we do not suffer as much from them. If infection and contagion were power, we would have just as many infectious and contagious diseases as the rest of the world. But we walk among them and nothing happens. Why? Because we have come to see that there is no power in infection or contagion. They could have power only if they were an activity of God. But they are not; they are just appearances tempting us to believe in an activity, a substance, or presence apart from God. What difference does it make whether it is a tiny germ or a great big bomb? Neither has the power to kill us! Only human belief gives them power.

If your life is threatened, smile at it because there is only One Life, and that is God's. Only your belief that there are two lives—yours and God's—subjects you to the fear of losing yours. But the moment you give up all sense of a life apart from God, you have entered immortality and eternality here on earth.

When we speak of Oneness, we are speaking of God as the Only Power—not as a power to be used over evil power or with which to overcome sin or disease, because there is no power out there to defend yourself against. In other words, "putting on the armor of Oneness" is like David going to meet Goliath without the world's sense of armor and without any of the world's weapons. David proved that Goliath was not a power but only a braggart.

"Putting on the armor of Oneness" means going out without the sword of offense or the armor of defense and without affirmations or denials. With affirmations and denials, we try to destroy sin, disease, death, lack, and limitation. But there is no reality to these conditions; they are only appearances that tempt us into battle.

First the battle is with armor and sword, then with guns and bombs; then as you become a metaphysician and go into the mental realm, the battle is with thoughts and affirmations and denials. It was easy to give up armor and swords when we were in that realm. But giving up affirmations and denials is more difficult.

Put on the armor of Oneness. Face every situation in life with that one word: *Oneness*. If you feel threatened by a bad activity, remember that God is the only Activity. If you are faced with a false sense of substance (too much or too little of it), remember that there is only one Substance and that is God. There is no evil substance; there is no bad substance; there is no sick substance. There is only one Substance, and that is Spirit.

Face every situation and every condition in life with the word *One*; One Life, One Soul, One Mind, One Being—even One Body. Since there is only one God and One Life, there can be only one embodiment, and that One is the body of God. Appearances indicate that each one of us has a body. We all seem to be different—some healthy, some not; some more, some less. And so we have accepted the belief in duality—more than one body.

"Know ye not that your body is the temple of the Lord?" That does not say that each one has a temple of God. It says that our body—yours and mine—is the temple of God. Since Oneness is the Truth, then there is only One Body, and there is nothing to fear about your body.

CHAPTER 7

PRACTICING SPIRITUAL TRUTH

Spiritual teaching plants seeds of Truth in your consciousness. Truth—a synonym for God, for Love, for the Christ, for the Spirit—is planted in our consciousness as a seed. Regardless of how profound the Truth may be, it can enter our consciousness only in the form of a seed. It is only a seed—not the fruit ready to eat, to enjoy, to share with our neighbors. You cannot share the seed itself. It would be like planting a seed in your garden and the next day digging it up to give it to your neighbor! If you did, you would never have a crop to share with your friends and neighbors and community.

It takes time for the seed to fulfill itself before it can become a full-blown realization. It must be buried deep in your consciousness and nurtured, fed, tended, cared for, and allowed to take root, to grow, to blossom, and to fulfill itself as fruitage that you can share. Do not look out the next day expecting to see a full-grown, fruit-bearing tree. Keep these gems of Truth locked up within yourself and witness how they develop and expand and come forth as fruitage.

The seeds of Truth that we take within our consciousness, live with, and practice over and over are our gratitude to God or to each other, our benevolences, forgiveness of our enemies, and praying for them. When these seeds of Truth come to fruition—when the Truth has been demonstrated within us—then we can begin to share the fruitage. The Truth has become a power to heal, to increase supply, and so forth.

We have the example of the Master who kept Truth locked up within Himself until the age of thirty. During that time He did not try to preach or teach or heal. He just pondered these Truths within Himself, lived with them, practiced them, was grateful for them. Then, when He was ready, He went out and demonstrated His spiritual Grace, which had become full-blown in Him.

Very often a Truth will reveal itself to us when we are reading a book or when we are meditating or even when writing. A Truth that we have known intellectually will suddenly become a living, vital, realized Truth. When that happens, we can go out and give it and find that we are giving it with signs following.

As many of you know, I never teach a Truth that has not been first realized and then demonstrated by me even though many books have been written about it. For many years students asked me about the Sermon on the Mount. My answer always was, "I have read it, but I don't understand it. It has not been realized, and therefore I will not comment on it." Then in 1956, while I was sitting on the platform giving a class, a full-blown realization of the Sermon on the Mount was given to me. During the rest of my 1956 classes I gave out this Truth that had revealed itself to me, because it was now a realized Truth, and the following year it was made public in my writings.

That is what we are supposed to do with the many Truths in the Bible. We have no right to speak of them until they come alive for us, live in us, and prove and demonstrate themselves. Then we have something from the Bible to share.

Nurturing Seeds of Truth in Secrecy

If something within you tells you that what I am saying is the fruitage of my experience and what I have witnessed in the lives of many on the spiritual path, if you feel any rightness in what I have said, then practice nurturing in secret one of the seeds of Truth. For example, take the principle of supply, keep it locked up within your consciousness, and begin to practice it in secrecy. Share even the little that you have. Cast your bread upon the water by finding some time each day to pray for and forgive your enemies and the enemies of the world. Find some period in each day for some kind of tithing. Practice the idea of even setting aside a specific amount of your income for whatever benevolences you wish to support. And *keep these things secret.* Remember to pray and do your benevolences in secret. If you do these things "to be seen of man" and thereby gain others' approval, you lose God's Grace. The Father, who sees in secret, will reward you openly.

Practice gratitude. Practice, "Thank you, Father. I have." Remember that if you express a lack, you will continue to experience that lack, because even the little that you have will be taken from you. "Whosoever hath not, from him shall be taken away even that he hath."[1]

Take into your consciousness these three words: Omnipresence, Omnipotence, Omniscience. Ponder them, and every time evidence of some erroneous form of power presents itself to you, realize within yourself that this erroneous form of power cannot be true if Omnipotence is true.

Whenever you are tempted to go to God to tell Him of your problems, immediately bring into thought the word *Omniscience*—All-Knowledge, All-Wisdom—and remind yourself that God already knows your needs and problems.

Work with these words conscientiously and continuously, but, above all things, do it silently and secretly. Talking about them will be like scattering the seeds on top of the earth instead of burying them in the earth.

Work with Omnipotence, Omniscience, Omnipresence until they grow in you and come forth as the full-grown babe. You will then understand that all conception is spiritual, that these ideas are conceived within you. Then you will understand the meaning of immaculate conception and virgin birth.

These ideas take root in you as embryos of Truth; and you work with them, ponder them, and rejoice over them until one day you will find these embryos of Truth come forth as virgin birth with signs following. They will come forth with joy and with singing. You will find that the wise men of the world will come to you and bow down to that Truth that has been born of you. Men and women will pay homage to you for this Truth that has been born in you and is now going forth from you into the world to bless it.

---

[1]Matthew 13:12.

However, before you can first present Truth to the world, you too may have to take it "down into Egypt and hide it" for a while, because the world always tries to destroy Truth. Why? Because Truth destroys the comfort of human life. Truth destroys material good as well as material evil. It destroys personal good and raises up in its place Divine Love, the love that we can share, not only with each other as members of a tiny religious group, but also with friends and even our enemies. We owe our neighbors Love regardless of their religious or medical beliefs.

Truth Can Be Uncomfortable

You will find that Truth makes people who are not searching for Truth very uncomfortable. As we come more and more to the spiritual way of life, we indulge less and less in the world's ways. Our language changes; curses and obscenities disappear from our vocabulary. The world's modes and means of living become more obnoxious to us than ever before. We are more offended by trifling injustices than the world is by major ones. And so it is that when you present Truth in any concrete form to those who still love this human life, be assured that you are offending them and they would "turn and rend you" unless you are wise enough to understand that no power has been given to any evil. All-Power is of God, and All-Power is good.

Too often we want to share the Truth we have with others when we see them in their distress. We feel that what we have could be so important to them that we rush out and try to share it with them. But when you are so tempted, please remember this principle of secrecy. Remember that you may gain your neighbor's goodwill but you will forfeit Divine Grace. Keep Truth within yourself until it has come to fruitage. Do not give forth the Truth that you know, but give forth only the fruitage: forgiveness, prayers, tithes. The secret is to keep it within you until it is so clearly established in you that you can share it freely and liberally.

Practice Truth in Every Activity

The trend of one's life can be changed within a year by studying, practicing, and living spiritual Truth. Practitioners can heal us once, twice, three times, even ten times and can feed us both spiritually and physically. But if we ourselves do not rise sufficiently in consciousness to embody Truth and to live Truth, we lose our opportunity to become free from sin, disease, lack, limitation, even death.

These freedoms cannot be attained without effort and struggle. It is not enough merely to read Truth or hear it. As Scripture tells us, we must become "doers" of the Word. We must study, practice, and live spiritual Truth, because Truth becomes demonstrable in our experience as outer harmony only in the proportion that it becomes an activity of our consciousness. The practice must be a daily, active part of our consciousness until it becomes a habit instead of only an occasional thought, treatment, or meditation.

My book *The Infinite Way* includes passages on pages 97 to 103 outlining an activity of Truth with which to start each day and, to some extent, carry on during the day. In the morning upon awaking, recognize God as the Activity of the day, as the Substance and the Law of all that will take place during the day. Recognize God as the One

Power and the One Presence that you will meet during the day.

This acknowledgement of God is in fulfillment of what Scripture tells us:

Thou wilt keep him in perfect peace, whose mind is stayed on thee: because he trusteth in thee. [2]

Trust in the Lord with all thine heart; and lean not unto thine own understanding. [3]

In all thy ways acknowledge him, and he shall direct thy paths. [4]

Thou shalt have no other gods before me. [5]

The practice of Truth applies to every activity and condition of our lives. Reading books on Truth, attending lectures or classes on Truth, and listening to recordings on Truth are fine activities as far as they go, but unless Truth becomes an activity of the conscious mind, it is not apt to produce lasting fruits.

We must make God the central theme of our lives by a conscious activity of thought. As we go out upon our day's work, we must realize that God is the Activity, the Source of our supply, the Law of our business, of our health, or our being—of all of our human relationships. God must be recognized as the actual source and avenue of our good. This has been a law throughout the ages since long before Abraham, Isaac, and Jacob. But it has been available only to those who practiced it. "Ye shall know the Truth, and the Truth shall set you free." But you must make it a

---

[2]Isaiah 26:3.
[3]Proverbs 3:5.
[4]Proverbs 3:6.
[5]Exodus 20:3.

conscious part of your awareness, a conscious part of your everyday living, until it becomes so automatic that you do far less conscious thinking about it. Then, of course, other phases of life follow, some of which you will find in my booklet *Love and Gratitude*.

Truth Is Hard Work

The practice of Truth is hard work, and I am the first to admit it. The Master said that the way is straight and narrow and few find it. Multitudes went to the mountain and witnessed the loaves and fishes being multiplied, and they were fed. But few among the multitudes could do the same. It was far easier to be fed by the Master than to learn how to do it themselves. The same was true of healing. It was far easier to let the Master do it. In the end, it was necessary for the Master to stop feeding the multitudes and healing the sick. He recognized that just having a full stomach or a well body was not getting anyone into the Kingdom of Heaven. Finally He said, "If I go not away, the Comforter will not come to you." Yes, multitudes sat at His feet and listened, but they would not go out and practice. Only about five hundred out of all the multitudes whom the Master taught and preached to learned enough Truth to recognize Him when He walked the earth after the resurrection!

Those who have been on the spiritual path will tell you that it is very hard to achieve one's spiritual freedom in Christ—freedom from material limitation, material law, moral limitation, all forms of limitation that hedge in the human being. They will also tell you that having achieved it, it is even more difficult to retain it, because the mesmerism of the world is such that succumbing to temptations becomes very easy. Each one of us may fall in a different way unless we consciously use every ounce of awareness we have to maintain and sustain our spiritual integrity.

You may ask, "If it's such hard work, is it worth the effort?" Anyone who has been healed of such conditions as an insufficient purse, insufficient health, or who has been a slave to false desires or appetites will tell you that it is well worth the struggle. Anything that can bring us better health, greater harmony, greater supply, or that can enable us to bring these freedoms to our family or friends or patients or students is worth working and striving for.

Studying and practicing music develops your musical consciousness, and studying art develops your artistic consciousness. In the same way, reading, studying, and practicing Truth develops your consciousness of Truth— your spiritual awareness of Truth. It is this spiritual consciousness that does the work. Once you have attained some measure of spiritual consciousness, you will no longer have to do much in the way of studying or treatment. It will be mostly a matter of maintaining that consciousness and holding it high above the mesmerism of the world by living and moving in spiritual consciousness.

The development of spiritual consciousness is possible for anyone on earth. The degree you attain depends entirely on how much time and effort you put into it. You cannot get more out of it than you put into it. The more you study Truth from teachers, from books, from recordings, from lectures or classes, the greater and quicker will be your development. But remember that all the studying and practicing leads to the attaining of some measure of spiritual consciousness, which does the work.

It is impossible for anyone to absorb and assimilate these principles upon learning of them for the first time. Therefore, avail yourself of every opportunity to hear them again or to read them again so that you can lock them up within you, ponder them, meditate them, and practice them until they bring forth fruit after their own kind. You will then truly be grateful for these lessons.

CHAPTER 8

THREE PRINCIPLES OF HEALING

There are three specific principles of The Infinite Way that we are to apply in meeting the problems of our everyday living. They also constitute the healing principles of The Infinite Way.

Probably the most important principle in the message of The Infinite Way is that we never use God for any purpose. We never use God nor do we use Truth to overcome sin, disease, or death. On the contrary, in The Infinite Way we seek to become the instruments of Truth. We open ourselves so that we may be used by God, by Truth. In other words, we seek to become the instruments through which God may manifest *Its*elf as our individual being and live *Its* life as us to guide, direct, govern, sustain, maintain, support, and supply.

God Uses Us to Heal

When we in our silence and stillness become in body and mind the instrument of God—the Infinite Love, the Infinite Wisdom, the Infinite Life—*It* can manifest *Itself* as us and perform *Its* functions through us. God or Truth can use us and can manifest *Itself* through us as healings if we have chosen the healing profession, as inventions if we are inventors, as music if we are composers, and so forth. Since God is Omniscience (Infinite Wisdom), all emanations are of God, whether they appear as engineering designs, scientific discoveries, literary works, or art works. Whatever form they take, they must be emanations of God since He is Infinite Wisdom and we are merely the instruments through which the Infinite Wisdom is manifested.

Therefore our approach to life is not learning how to use Truth or God, but how to be so receptive and responsive to the Divine Impulse that Truth can use us. Life can flow through us as our life, and Wisdom can flow through us as our wisdom. But it is not ours; it is God's.

God Is the Only Power

Afflictions, discords, diseases, and inharmonies exist in the human experience because of our ignorance of the basic Truth that God alone is Power. It is a universal ignorance, which takes over the moment we are conceived and begins to control us the moment we are born. We come into the world ignorant of spiritual Truth, accepting the belief in two powers—good and evil—long before we understand their meaning. We become deathly afraid of evil; we are afraid of falling, afraid of meeting strangers, afraid of automobiles, afraid of just about everything there is, and eventually we are sent to church and are taught to fear God!

As students of The Infinite Way, the first lesson we must learn is that since the nature of God is Infinite, no power or law belongs to anything of a discordant nature or material nature or limited nature. We must learn to "resist not evil," to "put up thy sword." We must learn to stand before every form of "Pilate" and say, "Oh, you look terrible and from what I hear about you, you are very frightening! But you could have no power over me unless it were given you by the Father."

It is difficult to come to the state of consciousness that can look at a crippled man and say, "What did hinder you? Pick up your bed and walk," or, "Lazarus is not dead, but sleeping. Come forth, Lazarus," or to the blind man, "Open your eyes and see," because there is no power to prevent it. There is only one power operating in consciousness, and that Power is God.

We must consciously make the transition to such a state of consciousness, because until this principle begins to come alive in us and becomes an inner conviction, we cannot demonstrate it. The transition comes with practice, and then of course we are able to demonstrate healing only in a measure.

That is the basic healing principle, and it gives students the most difficulty, especially metaphysical students, because they have been taught to use Truth to overcome error. You must get used to the idea that you, cannot use Truth, that Truth is Infinite, that Truth is God Itself. No one can use God, no one can influence God, and no one can get God to do his or her bidding. Have we unconsciously been thinking of God as a servant, telling God our needs and expecting God to fulfill them, telling

God what we want and expecting God to produce it, asking God for this favor or that favor or even commanding God as if He were a servant? The Master Himself acknowledged that He was not a master but the servant of God.

Evil Is Not Personal

We have another principle upon which healing work is based. Again, those of you with metaphysical backgrounds will have to work hard with it until you break yourselves of your former beliefs and come to understand this principle and demonstrate it. The principle is that *there is no such thing as personal evil.* You are not personally responsible for any of the sins, diseases, lacks, or limitations that come into your experience. Your wrong thinking did not produce it. Your envy or jealousy or malice did not produce it. Your greed or lust or mad ambition did not produce it. No fault that may be found in you produced it. You are not responsible for the evils that express themselves through you or in your experience. This is easy to accept; it becomes difficult only when I tell you that neither your wife nor your husband nor anyone else is responsible for any of the evils!

The Truth about you is that you are the child of God. God manifests *Its* own life as your individual being. God expresses *Itself* on earth individually as you. The Life that is God is your individual life, and it is therefore eternal and immortal. Your mind is the mind that was also in Christ Jesus, which is infinitely wise, infinitely pure. Your soul is spotless, and there is nothing you could ever do that would change that, because God is your soul, your very being. Going a step further, your body is the temple of the living

God. This is the Truth about you, about you life, your mind, your soul, your body, and your being. Why, then, all of these discords?

In ancient days an entity called Devil or Satan was created. Later, Paul called it "the carnal mind." In metaphysical language it is called the "mortal mind." It makes no difference what name you use; they are all correct. There is a Devil or Satan, and there is a carnal mind or a mortal mind, which is the source of all evil. Therefore, when you see a man stealing, do not call him evil, for he is only the instrument through which the carnal mind is operating. Regardless of what sin, disease, lack, or ignorance you witness in individuals, please do not condemn them. They are but the instruments through which the carnal mind is functioning. When Jesus was crucified, the Hebrews were blamed by some. The Romans were blamed by others. They were not to blame at all! It was the carnal mind, which is anti-Christ, against everything of God, and the carnal mind will destroy you if you recognize it as power.

Another mistake originally made was thinking of this Devil or Satan as the opponent of God and that it was God's function to get rid of this Devil or Satan. Down through the ages, religion has been dedicated to overcoming the Devil. But the Devil has no power! The Devil is nothing except what we make of it.

The metaphysical world has made the same mistake. Metaphysicians will tell you in any language that there is no Devil or Satan, that it is only the mortal mind. They then devise ways to protect themselves from the mortal mind, using all kinds of quotations and affirmations to overcome it!

We must recognize that all evil is impersonal. It comes from an impersonal source, and that source is the belief in good and evil. That is all there is to what is called the mortal mind. There is no such thing as mortal mind or carnal mind or Devil or Satan *as an entity*. There is only the universal *belief* in two powers, and that belief itself is the cause of every discord and inharmony that ever existed on the face of the earth.

Resist Not Evil

By battling the so-called mortal mind or any of its individual forms and expressions, you create an enemy greater than yourself. To the degree that you fight will you lose in the end because God, being too pure to behold iniquity, has no knowledge of it so He cannot help you with it!

The ancient Hebrews prayed, "God, please overcome my enemies; please destroy them; please go out before me and slay these horrible people!" These are not Christian prayers! Such prayers were not taught by Jesus Christ! But we do indulge in them, and even in metaphysics we do expect that God will overcome this mortal mind or this sin or this disease.

Overcoming the mortal mind must take place within you by your recognizing the Truth, "*I* will never leave you nor forsake you. If you go through the waters, you will not drown. If you go through fire, the flames will not kindle upon you." Why? Because they have no power. As you realize this, and as you realize the mission and the message of Christ Jesus, you will understand how He could forgive the woman taken in adultery or the thief on the cross or

Judas who betrayed Him. He knew by Divine Revelation that these had no power.

I know how difficult it is to look out at the sins and diseases and horrors of the world and actually believe that they have no power. But if you are able to accept and practice these spiritual principles until they become a living force within your own being, then when you witness your first healing, you will know that you have seen these principles in action. In other words, the first time you are instrumental in healing yourself or someone else without appealing to God to do something or expecting Truth to remove error but merely by realizing that God is the only Power and that "thou couldst have no power over me unless it were given thee of God," then you will have the conviction to go on and on until you are able to do the greater works.

Judge Not by Appearances

Humanly we have been taught to judge, criticize, and condemn anybody, any time, anywhere for anything that does not fit our own sense of what is right or wrong. But in this work you must change your entire attitude so that you are never guilty of judging, criticizing, or condemning a person. Instead, you must always recognize that the source of whatever appears to be wrong is only the carnal mind, which has no power, and that regardless of appearances, anyone who seeks help through spiritual means will receive it. This principle of "judge not after appearances" applies to everyone you meet in this life, whether or not they are seeking spiritual help.

Healing Is a Manifestation of Truth

Healing—whether it is the healing of insufficient health, insufficient supply, or some other condition—is the visible manifestation of the Truth of a spiritual message. That is why healing has been a major activity for me—not because of the importance of making sick people well, but because of the importance of revealing the principles through which we can be rid of ill health and find our spiritual health in God.

Healing is not done by knowing Truth only in an intellectual sense. It is not the Truth that you read, learn, or know that heals. Many who have thoroughly studied the many excellent textbooks on healing have not yet accomplished healing for themselves or for others, because healing is not done by the Truth you know. Healing is done by the consciousness of Truth that you attain.

When the Master was asked, "Art thou he that should come?" He answered, "The sick are healed. The dead are raised. Go show what thing ye have seen."

When we are asked, "Is The Infinite Way effective? Is it the Truth?" there is only one answer. "In proportion to the healings that you witness must it be judged." If you practice it faithfully, then we can say further, "You are demonstrating its truth in proportion to the healings that you achieve."

Two Steps in Healing

There are two steps in our healing practice: impersonalizing and nothingizing. We might say that there is a prior step—the realization of One Power and not trying to overcome negative powers or beliefs or claims that come before us—but that is a practice we embody at all times in our daily living. The two steps used specifically in healing or treatment are impersonalizing and nothingizing.

Impersonalizing

Your first function in healing work is impersonalization. The moment John Brown asks for help, be sure to put him out of your mind. Do not dwell on John Brown for one single moment. Above all, do not believe anything that is evil about John Brown; dismiss it instantly. The claim is not a condition, not a thing, not a person. It belongs to nobody. It is an impersonal imposition of what we might call the carnal mind or the mortal mind. See that it is not a person; it does not have a person in whom to work or through whom to work. Impersonalize it; take it out of the person.

When you are sure that you have impersonalized it so that you absolutely have no thought of the individual in your mind, then you take the second step, which is nothingizing.

Nothingizing

In Genesis we are told that God created all that was made, and all that He made is good. If God created all that was made, and all that He made is good, then He did not make the carnal mind or the mortal mind or Satan or the Devil. They are only mental concepts of the human mind. Anything that is not good, God did not make. Anything that God did not create does not exist.

If you want to know how powerless a human concept is, close your eyes now and in your mind build the largest atomic bomb you can possibly envision and combine it with hydrogen and all the forms of nuclear fission you have ever heard about. Now multiply it one thousand times. Then throw it up in the air and see what it can do! Nothing! It has no power. The bomb you have built in your imagination is only a mental concept. It has no substance, no law, no entity, no being. The only form it has exists only in your mind as a mental image.

Once you begin to understand that this Devil is a humanly created entity, made in the human mind and not in God's, and that it has no law, no substance, no activity, no source, no channel, then you nullify it. You have recognized it for what is it: temporal power, the arm of flesh, nothingness. That is where your healing work begins.

Regardless of the name or nature of the problem that confronts you, you can be assured that it is nothing but a temptation of the Devil coming to you for acceptance or rejection. It is nothing more than a human concept which exists because of a belief in good and evil. When you no longer believe in good and evil, you no longer have a human mind or mortal mind. There is limitation, finiteness, negativeness only as long as there is a belief in good and evil.

Wrong Thinking

Often when we are dealing with friends, relatives, or patients, we are apt to revert to a human sense of criticism or judgment or the metaphysical sense of saying, "It's your wrong thinking. There is something in your mind that must be corrected." Of course, there is, but the only thing that needs to be corrected is the belief in two powers. It is the same thing that has to be corrected in all of us—the belief that God is not Omnipotence, Omniscience, Omnipresence. The theory that resentment causes rheumatism, jealousy or envy causes cancer, and sensuality causes tuberculosis is a lot of nonsense! That is all it is—pure nonsense—because neither metaphysical nor psychosomatic medical practitioners can prove it. They can claim that when you get rid of the negative qualities of human emotions such as resentment, you will be healed, but they do not know how to get rid of them. But we know how: by understanding that they are impersonal and are not power and have no law to sustain them.

Every phase of discord that comes into our experience is a mesmeric influence from which we do not know how to protect ourselves. In other words, when you are in the midst of an epidemic of any disease, you are not necessarily suffering from the disease but from the mesmerism of the publicity about the disease. There are probably as many people dying of the mesmeric influence as of the disease itself. The same is true of catastrophic fires in tall buildings. We know that many who do not survive are victims of panic, fear, and lust for life and not from the flames themselves.

The universal belief in good and evil operates hypnotically upon every individual of this world. On any morning of the week the number of traffic fatalities can be predicted but not who will be the victims. It could be you or me. When you leave your home in the morning—what with coconuts falling from the trees and automobile accidents and lightning and this, that, and the other thing, you have no positive assurance you will return home in the evening. Is there a way to avoid becoming a statistic? Yes, indeed there is!

In the morning consciously realize:

There is but One Power operating in this universe, and it is not a power of accident, death, sin, or disease. The only Power operating is the same Power that causes the sun to rise and set and the tides to go in and out at their appointed times. It is the same Power that provides fish in the ocean and birds in the air. That is the only Power operating in this universe. That is the Power that is operating in my consciousness. That is the law unto my experience. There is no power in this mesmeric suggestion of statistics. There is no power in this belief of infection and contagion. There is no power in mortal mind, carnal mind, or any of its forms of belief, individual or collective.

Then you will see to what degree the ordinary, everyday mishaps stay outside of your experience. "A thousand shall fall at thy left and ten thousand shall fall at thy right hand, and it shall not come nigh your dwelling place." Whose dwelling place? The individual's who dwells in the secret place of the Most High—not in a house, not in an automobile, but dwells in the secret place of the Most High. How can you do that? It has to be done consciously.

Expressing Your Consciousness

Everything in your life is an expression either of your consciousness or of your unwillingness to let your consciousness express itself. When you block the expression of your consciousness, you become a blotting paper for the beliefs of good and evil that permeate the world. So you have a choice: you either become a blotter and take it all in and show it forth, or else you become a master of your fate and captain of your soul by an act of consciousness.

There must be an activity of Truth in your consciousness. That activity of Truth must be built no matter what form of treatment you give. It has to be built around the principle that there is only One Power, that only God and the activity of God is power, and that any sense of evil is impersonal and is nothing but the activity of the fleshly mind or nothingness. Every treatment must be built around these principles. No matter what the nature of the human claim is, it has to be consciously handled. Every treatment or realization must embody these two things: (1) the realization of One Power—not protection from evil power—but the realized knowledge that God is Infinite and only God is Power; and (2) the conviction that every appearance is but a mesmeric influence, a temptation of the Devil, which must be consciously rejected.

You will not bring harmony into your experience unless you live consciously in the realization of Omnipresent, Omnipotent, Omniscient God, the all and only Power, and then impersonalizing all phases of evil and realizing that evil exists only as the arm of flesh or nothingness.

When we are learning this principle, for a year or so it is hard work because we forget to live consciously in this realization more often than we remember. Try just a simple thing like this. Before you eat a bite of food or drink a drop of liquid, consciously recognize that God is the Source. At the end of the day count how many times you forgot to do so, and you will realize how difficult this is. If you do reach a point of consciously recognizing God as the source of every bite of food or drop of drink, you will experience magical effects in your life.

Come to the realization that the very trifling acts of your day—waking up in the morning, going to sleep at night—cannot be performed without an activity of God, an activity of the Invisible Spirit. See what happens as you begin to acknowledge Him in all your ways. See what happens as you consciously remember when you get into your automobile that God drives not only your car but—since there is only one Being, one Selfhood—all cars. Your conscious recognition of this sets you free from the belief in statistics.

This is difficult for a year or so, but eventually something beautiful happens. You no longer have to consciously think. It all comes to you with little or no conscious effort. The realization comes of its own accord; it flows from within you.

CHAPTER 9

PRINCIPLE OF TREATMENT

To receive or give treatment, you must consciously know and apply the principles of Truth. In order to do this, you must first establish dominion over your mind and your body.

Dominion over Mind and Body

We identify ourselves as "I." There is an "I," Joel; an "I," Mary; an "I," Bill—an "I," whatever your name is. But "I" is neither your body nor your mind. Your body and your mind are not the "I" of your being. They are merely the instruments through which you perform your functions on earth.

Your mind is the instrument through which the "I" of your being thinks, reasons, knows, and makes decisions and judgments. It is used for any purpose of awareness. Your body, on the other hand, is the physical instrument, which takes its orders from you (the "I") through your mind.

For example, when I wish to raise my hand, "I," Joel, through my mind give that order to my hand and my hand obeys. "I" govern my mind, and my mind instructs my body. Therefore, "I" have dominion over both my mind and my body. But suppose I do not exercise that dominion, which was given to me by God in the very beginning? If "I" exerted no control over my mind but let it make its own judgments, or if "I" let my body control its own conduct, I would be in all kinds of trouble, as are those who have not learned to accept and exercise their dominion.

Your mind and your body, as well as dominion over them, were given to you, and you must learn to exercise that dominion. When you sit in meditation, your mind does not wish to be still and come under control—not because it has a will of its own but because it is accustomed to doing what it wants if you have not been assuming dominion over it. The mind is much like some horses I have ridden, which did not acknowledge my control one bit! They just took me where they wanted to go because I did not know how to assume dominion over them, and so they had their way with me!

So the mind has its own way with us unless we learn to exercise dominion over it. In some respects, the body obeys more readily than the mind. At least your hands will not steal unless they are directed to do so, and they will share and give if you instruct them to do so. But in the matter of health, the body can be just as unruly as the mind. The body tries to determine for us whether we are well or sick. But we have as much dominion over health as we have over our minds or over morals. If we seem to have no dominion, it is because we have not assumed it.

Assuming Dominion Through Meditation

Since The Infinite Way teaches us that we must not take up the sword, we do not exert force to gain control or dominion over the mind and body. Instead, we use the same gentle, loving discipline that a wise, mature parent exercises over a child. It is a discipline of love, gentleness, peace, and patience. We gently and quietly address our minds in this manner ("I" am addressing my mind):

Peace! Be still! Fear not! God in the midst of thee is mighty. Fear not the armies of the world, for God in the midst of thee is mighty. God's peace give I unto thee. God's Grace give I unto thee. Peace! In quietness and in confidence shalt thou meditate. In stillness and in joy shalt thou receive God's Grace. Peace be unto thee! Peace! "My peace" give I unto thee.

You need not battle. You need take no thought for what you shall eat or what you shall drink or wherewithal you shall be clothed. God's Grace clothes thee. God's Grace feeds thee. Be still!

Be still and receive God's communion. Be still and hear the still, small voice!

You need not take thought. Be at peace! Be still! Nothing shall enter the mind that defileth or maketh a lie. No weapon that is formed against thee shall prosper, for where the spirit of Lord is, there is liberty, harmony, peace, quietness, calmness, assurance, confidence. In God's Presence is fullness of joy, fullness of life, abundance of good.

Here where I am, God is. I need not fear what mortals can do to me. They have only the arm of flesh. I have the Lord, God Almighty!

In this kind of meditation you take control of your mind and your body, and you realize that your identity (your "I") is apart from your mind and body, and "I" assumes jurisdiction over your mind and body. At the same time, you acknowledge that all this comes about not by virtue of any qualities of your own but by virtue of the Presence and Grace of God.

You will soon see the value of this when you are faced with a problem—either your own or one concerning someone who has turned to you for help, for you will then come into the subject of treatment.

Treatment As a Form of Prayer

Prayer itself is a spiritual activity. It is our communion with God. In its highest form, it is God's impartation of Himself to us. Both communion with God and God's impartation of Himself to us are prayer, and they are without words or thoughts. For many years the metaphysical world taught that treatment and prayer were synonymous. But that is true only in the sense that treatment is a form of prayer. I call it a much lower form of prayer because treatment is actually a preparation for prayer. Why is this?

The attainment of spiritual harmony is never accomplished by words or thoughts. Words and thoughts only help us to lift ourselves into that atmosphere of prayer where they are no longer necessary. In that atmosphere we are in an inner communion with God, and God's Grace reaches us.

We of the Western world cannot easily attain prayer without words or thoughts. However, we can rise to it through what metaphysics calls *treatment* and what orthodox religions call *prayer*. Both use words or thoughts and are often prayers of petition. For example, "God, send us rain for our crops!" "God, save my child!" There is nothing wrong with such forms of prayer any more than there is anything wrong with our forms of treatment. It is not a question of right or wrong. It is a question of degree of consciousness; as long as we are in a human state of consciousness, words and thoughts are necessary for us to begin our prayer work. The metaphysical world calls this *treatment*. The mystical world more often calls this *realizations*.

Students of The Infinite Way must not forget that they will rise into the true atmosphere of prayer and God-consciousness only by a thorough understanding and practice of the principles of treatment. Treatment means consciously knowing Truth and applying the principles in your mind after first establishing dominion over mind and body.

Treatment on Supply

Even in prosperous days, problems of supply are common. We will therefore address this problem. (If you have some metaphysical background other than The Infinite Way, it will be necessary for you to forget what you were taught, because on the subject of treatment The Infinite Way is not in agreement with any of the metaphysical movements. If you are having satisfactory results in some other work, be satisfied. Do not try to combine it with our work in The Infinite Way because you will not succeed and may find yourself worse off than you are at the moment.)

To begin with, under no circumstances do we take the patient into our treatment. We never take the patient's name into our thoughts. As a matter of fact, if a patient does not give us a name, we do not even ask for it. We are not interested in patients' names or identities. Our work has nothing to do with them, although they will receive the fruitage of it. "How," you may ask, "do they receive the fruitage of it instead of everybody else?" Because *they* have brought themselves to our consciousness and made themselves a part of it by asking for our help.

> *Thy faith hath made thee whole.* [1]

> *Believe ye that I am able to do this? . . .*
> *According to your faith be it unto you.* [2]

To whom you submit yourself, them will you obey and from them will you receive. So if a patient says to you, "Give me help," the necessary contact has been made with you even if you do not know the patient's name or identity or what he or she looks like.

Remember that the person must not enter the treatment because that act will be a barrier against the success of your treatment. You must not under any circumstances take the person into your thoughts. Neither can you take the "claim" into your meditation. You cannot take lack or limitation into your consciousness, because you cannot in any way work on the level of the problem.

When the problem is one of supply, there is only one thing that you can do. You can turn from that person and

---

[1]Mark 5:34.
[2]Matthew 9:28–29.

from that problem and immediately begin to consciously know the Truth—not the Truth about the problem because there is no truth about it. The first thing that must reach your consciousness (not necessarily in these words but in similar passages of Scripture or metaphysical or mystical language) is the Truth about supply:

> The earth is the Lord's and the fullness thereof. God constitutes the fulfillment of all being. God is the only supply. God does not belong to anybody. The earth does not belong to anybody. There is no one who can get supply. This earth is God's footstool, and all that is therein. God constitutes this universe. God's Presence fills this universe. God is the only Life and the only Law unto this universe.

As you in this manner consciously dwell on the Truth about supply, you will remember more and more passages bearing out the fact that God alone is supply. "I am the bread, I am the meat, I am the wine, I am the water." Since God is omnipresent (filling all space) and God is supply, where is the lack? The absence of supply is with those who do not abide in the Word and do not let the Word abide in them. The lack is with those who do not dwell in the secret place of the Most High, and with those who are cutting themselves off from the only supply there is: the Word of God, the bread, the meat, the wine, the water, the realization of God's Presence.

As you can see, your treatment consists of your consciously knowing the Truth about what constitutes supply and about the fullness of God and His Omnipresence. You take into your consciousness statements of Truth, passages of Scripture. Your treatment is on the level of spiritual Truth, not on the level of the problem of lack or limitation.

Keeping your patient and the problem out of your consciousness and keeping your treatment on the Truth, you will eventually run out of thoughts and words and scriptural passages. You will have raised yourself into the atmosphere of prayer where words and thoughts are no longer necessary.

In The Infinite Way we are unique in that we do not consider this initial stage of any value in and of itself. It is only a stepping-stone to the second part of our treatment. It is only the preparation for the second stage when we can say, "It is your turn, Father. Speak, Lord, thy servant heareth." This second phase is a period of waiting and listening, of expectation of the inner peace, that "click," that something through which you know that God is on the field. This is not a mental declaration. It is a spiritual realization. When you inwardly experience this, your work is complete and you can go about your business.

Your patient's problem may be an obstinate one, especially if your patient is one who believes that he or she can add God's Grace to a life lived on a worldly level. Too many in the metaphysical movement really believe that all they need to do is attend a lecture on Truth or find the right practitioner to say or do the right thing and then the blessings of God will come to them.

Many do have several wonderful demonstrations or healings, but later they find that the treatments no longer work. They have benefited by the practitioner's state of consciousness, but if they have not yielded themselves to God, they eventually find that the treatments no longer work. In other words, the practitioner through his or her own dedicated life can free a patient from many trials and tribulations, sins and diseases, lacks and limitations. But heaven help the patient who goes on in the same old human way for very long, because he or she will find that the treatments no longer work! The Master gave this principle to us when He said, "Neither do I condemn thee, but *go and sin no more.*"

A patient may have several wonderful demonstrations or healings before achieving a transformation of consciousness. But the patient must eventually yield the self to God; he or she must yield mortal sense in order to make room for spiritual awareness. The patient must undergo some kind of spiritual regeneration; otherwise he or she will find that the treatments no longer work.

Paul taught us that human beings cannot receive God's Grace because they are not under the law of God and cannot be. Only if we permit the Spirit of God to dwell in us is it possible to become the child of God. "If so be the Spirit of God dwell in you, then are you the son of God." Jesus gave it to us in another way: "Pray for your enemies that ye may be children of God." Pray not for your friends or relatives, but *pray for your enemies.*

The Spirit of God does not dwell in a person filled with envy, jealousy, malice, hate, revenge, and so forth. When you achieve a state of consciousness where you can honestly and sincerely pray that your enemies be forgiven, that they be released from punishment for their sins, that they be released from these mortal claims, that the Spirit of God enter their souls, their minds, and their being, then you are no longer a mortal. If you are in a state of consciousness where you still want revenge, where you still think that sinners should be hung or placed in solitary confinement or jailed for life, where you believe that so-and-so had it coming, then you are in the ancient Hebrew state of consciousness that seeks "an eye for an eye, and a tooth for a tooth." But when you make the transition to Christhood, you are able to forgive seventy times seven, to resist not evil, and to take not up the sword. In that state of consciousness you yield your will, your opinions, and your convictions; you accept the Grace of God, the Spirit of Christ. Then the Spirit of God does dwell in you.

If you honestly feel that you have yielded whatever negative human emotions you may have been indulging in, you can know not only that you are now in an atmosphere that is receptive and responsive to spiritual healing, but also that you are approaching the consciousness that can do healing work.

A title or a degree or an authorization does not make a healer. Many totally unprepared people go into healing work. "By their fruits you shall know them." The healer is one who has yielded up his or her humanhood, who is free of antagonism, hate, envy, jealousy, malice, and other negative emotions, and who has attained the state of consciousness where he or she forgives seventy times seven and can pray for enemies, put up the sword, and resist not evil.

When we have yielded and the Christ has filled our consciousness, then we are prepared to be healed spiritually and to heal others.

I have found that in every one of the metaphysical movements there are practitioners who have attained enough of Christ-consciousness to be able to heal. It makes no difference whether they belong to The Infinite Way or to Christian Science or to Unity or to New Thought. What determines their healing ability is the degree of spiritual consciousness they have attained.

Treatment for a Physical Claim

The next request for help may be for a physical problem. The patient's claim may be that the organs or muscles or bones or blood vessels are not functioning properly. Before starting your treatment, remember that you must wipe out from your consciousness not only the patient but the claim as well. Since you are not a physician, it does not matter to you whether it is the heart, liver, or lungs.

Your treatment has to do only with knowing the Truth, and there is no Truth about your patient or the claim. A patient has a pain in his chest, and immediately it is heart disease. Another patient discovers a lump, and immediately it is cancer. The patient then perpetuates it by holding it in his or her thoughts. So for you to give thought to the claim when giving a treatment is non-sensical.

Forget the identity of the patient, and forget the claim as fast as it is unloaded on you. In my office there are no records of who came or who called. The only time a name appears on my calendar is when I have a future appointment. There are no other names, no record of treatment, no bills to be sent, no record of claims, no case histories.

After wiping from your consciousness the patient's identity and the claim, you proceed in the same way as with treatment for a problem of supply. In the first stage you take into your consciousness statements of Truth, passages of Scripture, or metaphysical or mystical statements of Truth. You begin to consciously know the Truth—not about the claim, because there is no truth about it, but the Truth that in the entire Kingdom of God there is no trace of sickness. Again, the statements of Truth that reach your consciousness are not necessarily the ones that follow. I am giving them merely as examples.

Christ's healing ministry was, "What did hinder you? Pick up your bed and walk. Lazarus, come forth! Thou art not dead; thou sleepest!"

In the entire Kingdom of God there is no trace of sickness. God did not create sickness; God created only good. God is the only Creator. Therefore humans cannot even create disease or illness; humans merely *believe* in the power of illness or disease.

If there were such a thing as sickness that eventually leads to death, there would be no immortality, no eternality.

The Kingdom of God is immortality, eternality, life, love. The Kingdom of God is a Kingdom of Grace, not of law. Therefore there can be no laws of matter, of mind, of weather, of climate, of food, of limitation.

The Kingdom of God is a state of Grace.

As in treatment on the problem of supply, as you consciously dwell on statements of Truth, other passages of Scripture will enter your consciousness until you eventually run out of thoughts or words. You will have lifted yourself into the atmosphere of prayer where they are no longer necessary, and you will now be able to sit back and say, "Father, it is your turn. Speak, Lord, thy servant heareth." You then enter the second stage where you await the inner spiritual realization that God is on the field. When you inwardly experience this, your work is complete.

Not once has your mind dwelled on the patient or the claim. You have tabernacled with God and kept your conversation in Heaven.

Remember the hymn, "I Will Listen for Thy Voice." It is not a mere hymn; it is a spiritual state of being. In a few moments of quiet and peace, something will come to you within, some feeling, some words, some message, some light; and you will know that God is on the field.

CHAPTER 10

TEMPORAL POWER IS NOT POWER

To the transcendental consciousness, temporal power (whether it is of a physical nature or of a mental nature) is not power. The only power is the realized consciousness of the One Power and recognizing the nonpower of all else.

When Hezekiah's people came to him and said, "The armies of the enemy are upon us and they are greater in number than we are," he replied, "Be not afraid! They have only temporal power, the arm of flesh. We have the Lord, God."

The Master could say to Pilate, the great temporal power of that time, "Thou couldest have no power at all against me, except it were given thee from the Father."

Take unto yourself the task of understanding what these two passages mean. Could you, right now, turn your face toward a hostile country and in your honest, open heart say, "You have no power over me," or, "You have only temporal power, the arm of flesh"? Could you say that and actually feel completely and perfectly safe? Of course not, and you will not be able to until you understand that temporal power is not power. To the degree that you attain a confidence and assurance in Omnipotence, you will know that temporal power is not power.

The Principle of No-Power

Some of you who have done healing work have achieved to some degree this transcendental consciousness. None of us has achieved the fullness of it, but everyone who has done spiritual healing work has been able to say to infection, contagion, or disease, "You have no power," and has seen them dissolve. Everyone who has been an instrument for healing has proven that in the Presence of God temporal power is not power. There is no power but the realization of God's Presence, and we have proved it in the knitting of fractured bones, in the healing of blindness and deafness. We have proved again and again that temporal power is not power.

In the human world there are many temporal powers: those of disease, sin, money, politics, war, and so forth. If you pray in the nonsensical manner of the past, "God, overcome my enemies or overcome those atomic bombs," you are wasting precious time, because God has never done so and never will. God does not do something to an evil power. God is not a power *over* another power. God simply *is* the Only Power, the All-Power. Prayers have failed in the past because they have tried to overcome a temporal power, which is not a power. It is like trying to overcome a mirage in the desert. How can you exert power over something that does not exist? In the past prayer has been used to exert spiritual power over other powers, but there are no other powers.

Do not pray God to destroy any enemy, not even the enemies we call sin and disease. Do not think of God as a great power that will go out and do battle with sin, disease, lack, limitation, and death. Rather, look upon God as Spirit, Life, Love, always where you are, and filling all space. Then seek a greater awareness of what the Kingdom of God is, what the supply of God is, what the companionship of God is, and what the household of God is. While you are tabernacling with God, witness how the affairs around you are falling into place without your taking thought about them. When you attain the realization that what appears as an evil power is not power, harmony will appear in your experience.

Realize that *My Kingdom*, the Christ Kingdom, is not of this world, and yet *My Kingdom* is the Only Power of any world. Then, when you are presented with an appearance of evil (whether it is in the form of sin, disease, war, discord, communism, capitalism, or whatever -ism you don't like), ask yourself, "Is this spiritual power? Is this a God-Power?" Of course not! God is too pure to behold iniquity; there cannot be an evil power of God. God sent forth the Master to show the nothingness of sin, disease, lack, and death. No sin, no disease, no lack, no war could ever emanate from God. Therefore, this appearance of evil you are faced with must be only temporal power. Once you recognize it as merely temporal power, you will realize that this means it has no power, because that which is not of God is not power. What you are faced with only appears as effect and is temporal. Spiritual power is invisible; God, the All-Power, is invisible. Therefore, any danger that is so very visible cannot be power and cannot be of God.

The Power of Evil Is Not Real

As you begin to recognize the nature of evil, you will understand that the nature of prayer is not the overcoming of evil, and you will quickly change the entire experience of your life.

Evil is not ordained of God. It has no law of God to sustain it. It has no God-existence or God-purpose. It is therefore temporal, the arm of flesh, or nothingness. The moment you realize this, you no longer resist evil. Remember that as long as you are praying for a God-power to overcome evil, you are resisting evil and are trying to use that power to help you do so.

Instead of trying to resist or overcome evil, relax and say, "All right, Father, stay in your heaven. I don't need you right now because what is facing me is only a mirage, not a power. If a real power comes along and the going gets rough, I will call on you. But this isn't a power."

You need not fear what mortal humans can be, think, or do to you. You need not fear mortal power, temporal power, material power. You need not fear infection, contagion, disease, or age, because nothing in the realm of effect is power. All power is invisible, and that which is appearing as power is only a mental image, a mistaken concept of power. You must know this Truth, and this Truth will set you free. But, while you are knowing this Truth, remember that to some extent your life must bear witness to the experience. In other words, you cannot deny the power of effect while hating or fearing somebody because they are part of that effect. You must make your thoughts and actions conform to your treatment.

Do not be disheartened if you cannot do it 100 percent of the time. Occasionally you will fail because it is impossible to change overnight from material sense to complete spiritual consciousness. The change cannot come with only one, two, or three years of studying and meditating. Be grateful that from the moment you begin to practice this principle, you are attaining in some measure the mind that was in Christ Jesus, and to that same degree you are outwardly demonstrating the fruitage of it. Be very patient with yourself.

Every fall and early winter you hear more about flu, grippe, infection, contagion, epidemics, and so forth. You may already be at the state of consciousness where those things do not come nigh your dwelling place. But for the sake of your community and your world, you will need to remember every day that this is temporal power—no power. It is not of God; therefore it has no existence except as a mental concept erroneously given power.

There is only one mind that is God's, and that cannot be the carnal mind. The mind that is God's is the mind that was in Christ Jesus. Therefore, the carnal mind and its activities are not power; they are only the arm of flesh and are not to be feared. As you experience that inner feeling of relief from fear, you release the power of God in the world.

The activity of the carnal mind appears in many forms. It may appear as juvenile delinquency one day, as drug dealing or as child molesting another day, and so forth. It will appear in one form or another, but do not believe for a moment that it will be erased until there are such as we who will not fight it but sit back and realize that this is only the carnal mind. It has appeared in every age and in every generation, and its forms will continue to appear until groups like ours begin to demolish them—not by fighting the specific evils or the specific groups, but by realizing that they are merely forms of carnal mind, another form of no power, only temporal power, the arm of flesh, or nothingness. As you experience that inner feeling of release from fear and concern, you again release the power and Presence of God into this universe.

My Kingdom

Keep the two words My Kingdom with you always. My Kingdom means the Christ Kingdom. Keeping those two words in mind, realize that the temporal universe is not to be feared or hated or loved. It is an illusion; and right where it seems to be, My Kingdom, the Kingdom of God, is. My Kingdom is the reality. What your eyes see or your ears hear is the superimposed counterfeit that is a temporal concept, a concept of temporal powers. My Kingdom is intact; it is the Kingdom of God; it is the Kingdom of the children of God; My Kingdom is here and now. All that exists as a temporal universe is without power. You need not fear it or hate it or condemn it. You need only to understand it.

You will witness in many ways that this world and its forms of sickness, its forms of sin, its forms of false appetites, its forms of lack and limitation will begin to disappear. In place of these you will find harmonious conditions and relationships, and this shows forth your higher state of consciousness.

Your state of consciousness is the hub of it all, because your world is the externalization of your state of consciousness. As ye sow, so shall ye reap. If you sow to the flesh, you will reap corruption, sin, disease, death, lack, limitation. If you sow to the spirit, you will reap life everlasting. By the word *sow* we mean "being conscious of." If you are conscious that My Kingdom, the spiritual kingdom, is the real kingdom and what the five senses bear witness to is without power, is temporal, is the arm of flesh, then you are sowing to the spirit, and you will reap harmony in body, in mind, in purse, in human relationships. But if you continue to fear "man whose breath is in his nostrils," if you continue to fear the political organizations of the world, if you continue to fear infection, contagion, and epidemics, you are sowing to the flesh. If you realize that all power is in the Invisible, you are sowing to the spirit, and you will reap divine harmony.

The moment you think of prayer or treatment or meditation, instantly think in these terms: "My *Kingdom*, the Christ Kingdom, is power. The temporal kingdom— all that we see, hear, taste, touch, or smell—is not power; it is not of God." Eventually you will have the inner peace that assures you that you have prayed aright, and there will be signs following. Train yourself to realize that the temporal world is only temporal power, and temporal power is not power; it is an arm of flesh. "This is but the arm of flesh; we have the Lord God Almighty," really means that "this" is not power. The only power is the Invisible, which *I* really am, and *I* am invisible.

So it is with your body. It is visible; therefore, it has no power. It cannot be well or sick. The Power is in you— whether you are sowing to the flesh or whether you are sowing to the spirit—because when Scripture says, "I create good, and I create evil," that I is the human you or me. We create the only erroneous conditions in our experience by whether we are accepting God as Omnipotence, Omnipresence, Omniscience or whether we are still accrediting power to the temporal universe.

We create our own world by whether or not we are sowing correctly. "As ye sow, so shall ye reap," means only one thing: Are you making yourself conscious of God as the reality, as the only Power, as the only Law? Or are you continuing to live in this finite world, accepting its belief in two powers, two presences, two laws, two causes? We change our world when we consciously make the decision that we will live in the conscious realization of God as being the only Power, the only Law, the only Cause. We change our entire world as we look out and behold the finite world and realize, "Since you are only effect, the power is not in you. The power is not in this hand of mine. The power is in the *I* that I am. *I* directs it and the rest of my body. If I realize that, then the body cannot talk back to me. *I* am talking to it, and *I* am reassuring it that *I* am its life, *I* am its intelligence, *I* am its substance, and *I* am its law—meaning the *I* that I am." Then the body has to obey. But if we believe that this body has power, we are giving power to the temporal universe, we are giving power to the arm of flesh.

As you practice this principle, you will find that more and more your attention will be on *My Kingdom* and *Thy Grace* rather than on form and effect. You will be thinking now in terms of spiritual Grace, spiritual harmony, spiritual relationships—not better human relationships, not better human health, not just dollars or other currency. These do not constitute spiritual harmony or spiritual growth, although they are the effects of spiritual harmony and spiritual growth. You will find yourself no longer thinking in terms of a better material body or looking for material good. You will be absent from the body and present with the Lord; and as you do this you will find that body, form, and effect appear harmonious.

God Is Not a Power to Be Used

God-power is not to be invoked by humans, and it is not attained by influencing God in our behalf. It is not a power over sin, disease, or death any more than light is a power over darkness. The truth is that there is no such thing as darkness. Darkness is only an absence of light. It is not a presence; it is not an entity; it is not a substance that you can examine under a microscope. You cannot capture a piece of darkness and examine it, because there is no such thing as darkness. Darkness is merely the absence of light.

Sin, disease, and death—like darkness—do not exist, because what God did not create does not exist, for He is the only creating, maintaining, and sustaining power. In Genesis we find, "God looked upon all that He made and found it good." It is not in His nature to look upon sin, disease, and death and find them good; therefore He could not have created them.

Another point is that what God created is forever; He would not let anyone disrupt anything He had created. If He had created sin, disease, and death, there would be no hope of our overcoming them.

We do not need God-power to overcome something that was not made in the beginning, never had existence, and represents only our ignorance of the Truth. Your healing power, then, which is your spiritual power, rests only in your knowing the truth that God is the All-creating, maintaining, and sustaining power and that what He did not create does not exist. Therein lies your only spiritual power.

World Peace

The world has but one hope for peace, and it is that we in The Infinite Way make the demonstration that temporal power is not power. The world has gone too far on the road to ultimate material power, in developing destructive weapons, for peace ever to be negotiated. As spiritual students, do not believe for a moment that any human being or any political party on earth has the answer to peace. The world has gone too far for any human solution. There is a spiritual solution, which will remove danger and all thought of war—hot or cold—from the world. It is this.

We must see that temporal power is not power, that it is but the "arm of flesh" while we have the Lord, God Almighty. The Lord, God Almighty, is the only power that anyone has, the only power, the All-Power. No one has an exclusive on it. At this moment we of The Infinite Way have an exclusive on the understanding of this particular truth and its demonstration. But, as we continue to demonstrate it in our experience, we are going to experience it for the world, because that is all it will take to end the world's problems: the realization that temporal power is not power and not resisting it, not trying to overcome it, not fighting it, but just quietly resting in the realization of its nothingness.

In the same way, if a member of your family were taken ill, you would be compelled to sit by the person and say to yourself, "I will not believe in temporal power. I will not give power to this disease (or this sin or this false appetite)." As you sit there realizing, "This is temporal power, which is no power," you will find your relative (or friend or neighbor) getting better. Then you will know that you have proven, if only in a small way, that temporal power in any form is not a power. That is the key to healing. It is the healing principle. There is no other key.

As humans we could not have peace even among ourselves because there is bound to be envy, jealously, or malice springing up. We can have peace among ourselves as we individually abide in the realization that *My Kingdom* reigns here—not human good, not human evil—just *My Kingdom,* the Kingdom of God. If there is any human evil among us, it is not power. It is not person, so it cannot manifest itself and it has to die of its nothingness. If there is any evil, any sin, any hate, envy, jealousy, or malice, what of it? It is only temporal; it is impersonal. It is forever without person in whom, on whom, or through whom to manifest. It is the arm of flesh or nothingness. We have the Lord, God Almighty, the Divine Love, the Divine Wisdom—the only Wisdom—operating among us. Not human intelligence, not human love, not human gratitude, but the Presence and the Power of God.

Think in terms of the room you are in. Imagine if you can that if any evil, any disease, or any poverty is there, it is temporal, temporary, not of God, a nothingness. You have the Lord, God Almighty, as the Life, Mind, Soul, and Being—even the body. The body is the temple of God, and do you not see that this is the healing agent?

The next step is letting your thoughts spread out to your community and realizing that if any evil is there, what of it? It is impersonal; it is the carnal mind; it has no divine law to maintain it or sustain it. See how quickly conditions improve! However, if you are not putting this principle into practice, the principle will not come true in your experience, for there is no mysterious God sitting up there to do it for you. *Ye* shall know the Truth, and the Truth shall make you free. You have to bring that truth into experience in your individual affairs, collective affairs, city, national, and world affairs.

The Burdens Will Be Lighter

It is not beyond possibility for humans to live by the activity of the Christ, because living by the activity of the Christ is the normal and natural way. The human way, which is brought about by what is called in religious language "human disobedience or human falling away from Grace," is the unnatural way. This unnatural way is the reason man has to live by the sweat of his brow and woman has to bring forth children in pain and travail.

Under the activity of the Christ there is no pain to childbirth. Whenever a practitioner of spiritual capacity is in attendance, childbirth is painless. By that, I do not mean that anybody who calls himself or herself a practitioner can do it—any more than such a practitioner can heal! But when childbirth is attended by a practitioner who has attained a measure of the Christ, it becomes natural and painless. This example is only one evidence of what I mean by living by the activity of the Christ.

We are not meant to live by the grace of "man whose breath is in his nostrils." We are not meant to be dependent on husbands or wives or estates. We are not meant to live by taking thought for what we shall eat or drink or wherewithal we shall be clothed. We are not meant to live by worry, concern, fear, or doubt. We are meant to be concerned only with showing forth God's glory. Every act of our lives should show forth the fact that God is functioning in our lives.

The moment we take responsibility for ourselves and start planning, we shut off the activity of the Christ. On the other hand, when we refrain from taking thought or making a move, we make way for the Christ to act, and we carry out on the human plane whatever is given us to do. In other words, we say to ourselves, "All right, today I will do whatever prompting comes to me each hour." For example, when I leave here, my next thought may be to have lunch. Well, then, let it be lunch! However, it may well be that while I am concentrating on lunch, a telephone call comes and I have to postpone lunch. Now, if I permitted my plans to govern my actions, nothing would thwart my having lunch, and I would not be doing what is given me to do at that particular time. If you realize always that you are subject to the One Power that is Christ, some incident may arise that will prevent your doing what you had planned. So you do whatever is given you to do at that moment, then go on to the next activity. Each step of the way we wait, and the Christ functions, and we then carry out what is given us to do at that moment.

If we awaken one morning and all day the right things are said at the right time, the right acts are done at the right time, the right people come into our experience at the right time, and the wrong people are eliminated from our experience at the right time, then we can see that every phase of our experience is a direct result of the activity of the Christ. We are not really doing it; we are not even taking thought about it. *It*, the Christ, is living our lives before we have any awareness of it.

As long as the human mind is feverishly active, the Christ cannot break through and reveal *Itself*. We are a nation of go-getters. We do not know that the best way to accomplish anything is to have long, frequent periods of quiet, doing nothing and getting nothing. That is when we receive the inspiration that makes it possible for us to accomplish more in one hour than we can humanly do in twenty-four hours. The person who has the knack of being mentally quiet accomplishes more in less time than the person who cannot be mentally quiet. And the person who goes the next step higher and opens herself or himself to the activity of the Christ is without limit! There is no limit to what the Christ can perform in twenty-four hours through a human being. There is absolutely no limit!

Recently a college student wrote to me for help. She had been so busy with her many college activities, she was afraid she would not pass her examinations. Later she wrote that she passed her examinations with perfect grades. Not some of them, but all of them and not with mere passing grades, but with perfect grades. This would not have been possible for a human being, but it was possible to the activity of the Christ, because *It* takes no thought for what your capacity is. *It* operates through *Its* capacity; you are only the instrument.

Recall the temple gate Beautiful in Acts and visualize Peter and John raising the crippled man. Neither Paul nor John could have done any such thing! There had to be an activity beyond their human capacity. They acknowledged it when they said, "Ye men of Israel, why marvel ye at this? . . . as though by our own power or holiness we had made this man walk."[1]

It is not false modesty that makes a practitioner say, "It was not my understanding or my power," when a healing takes place—whether it is a simple headache or cancer or consumption (tuberculosis) or paralysis. Being praised for such a healing is just as ridiculous as receiving the Medal of

---

[1]Acts 3:2.

Honor when you were not even there! But let us not forget that if the practitioner had not attained that degree of humility, that which healed could not have done it! Never forget that the impotent or paralyzed man at the temple gate Beautiful would still be sitting there if there had been no Paul or John of sufficient selflessness to permit the activity of the Christ to function. Jairus's daughter and Peter's mother-in-law and Lazarus would still be where they were if there had not been someone of a sufficient degree of nothingness to permit the Infinity to appear and heal through them. That is the secret of this work.

Some years ago, the writer William Saroyan wrote that he was convinced that God lives our lives and we just go along for the ride. At a certain stage of unfoldment, that is exactly true. We are on this plane only as witnesses. We witness coconuts growing on trees and roses blooming and grass growing after it has been cut, but we have done nothing to bring it about. It is true that we are prompted to water and fertilize the lawn, but in doing so we are only doing what is given us to do. *He* performeth what is given me to do. *He* tells me, then I have a feeling that I ought to water or fertilize the lawn. Or I may have a feeling I ought to go to town today to take care of certain things that have been waiting for weeks to be done, yet never before did I have an urge to do them. Or something may lie on my desk for days and even weeks without my being able to do anything about it. One day *It* says, "Now!" Then the work is done in that minute, and I find that everything has worked together toward that minute when the work is done "in a jiffy!"

You have experiences when you clearly know that you have shown forth an activity of the Christ. In other words, when you have had a healing of a headache or a sore throat or a footache and have known for certain that the healing was not brought about by any human means or by waiting for a human healing time, then you knew that it was the activity of the Christ. Or perhaps some other problem of relationship or supply was met so dramatically that you knew beyond doubt that nothing of a human nature brought it about but that it was the activity of the Christ that produced it.

However, these experiences represent only living between visitations of the Christ, or from one visitation to another; whereas the Christ is a spiritual Presence and Power that takes over *every* function of your life. *It* takes over the functions of the body so that you do not have to take thought for walking, talking, remembering, digesting, or eliminating. You do not have to help it in any way, because the activity of the Christ, the Spirit within, takes over these functions. If I have to take thought for getting my blood to circulate or my digestive or eliminative organs or my muscles to function, then I am living by bread alone and not by every word that proceedeth out of the mouth of God. But when my body is functioning without my taking any thought about it—and without even knowing that I have a blood system or digestive or eliminative system—then it is the direct evidence of Christ in action.

I am telling it very imperfectly; but what I am trying to say is that from this day forward do less yourself and watch more being done by the Activity. Be a witness to the Christ activity. Be a beholder! See if you can detect things taking place in your life about which you can say, "Ah, I know that that is an activity of the Christ because I had nothing to do with it. I never even thought about it! I never dreamed of such a thing coming into my experience!

Yes, that was an activity of some invisible Presence and Power that was operating on my behalf."

You can see the Activity in the experience of those around you. It is especially obvious in the case of children and those who are still innocent of the world's ways. You find yourself doing things for them that you had not planned or expected to do. You may not realize it, but when this happens you are responding to the Christ that is governing their lives. The Christ is functioning for them and using you for their benefit. The Christ activity is also functioning on behalf of a pet dog. *It* uses us to feed and house a pet animal and to supply its needs. Pets have an invisible, protective, maintaining, sustaining influence, and we are being used by that influence in the same way we are being used in the case of children. They have an inner something that sees to it that they are provided with food, clothing, shelter, and entertainment without their taking any thought for the cost of these things or how hard it is to get the money to pay for them. They just need something and it is provided for them through you. You find that you even inconvenience yourself or do without so that they may have these things, not realizing that you are being an instrument of the Christ that is operating in them and for them.

Christ in action is the Activity of the body, of the purse, and of our relationship with each other. The Presence goes before us to prepare a place for us and to make the crooked places straight, and everything is done for us.

Christ is God *Itself* in *Its* individual expression in our lives, just as the sun is the whole sun yet is centered or individualized in this particular area. A thousand miles from here that same sun is shining as an individual sunbeam, yet it is the entire sun itself. In the same way, God is the Christ; God constitutes the Christ. God is the universal Infinite Allness expressing *Itself* individually as your consciousness and mine in the proportion that we permit it to by relaxing from taking conscious thought.

How much lighter our burdens are when the Christ activity is operating in our experience! It may not have been operating heretofore, but today we have the promise that the activity of the Christ will be more evident than it has been heretofore, if we permit it. However, we must always be alert whenever we are doing anything to ask ourselves, "Am I doing this, or is the Christ doing it?" If you cannot feel that the Christ is doing it, stop!

In today's human world very few people can be alone or silent or still. Modern life continuously distracts the human mind. The mind is distracted by outside noises of planes overhead or trains rolling by, or it is occupied with movies, television, bridge games, even solitaire. Something has to be going on in the external realm to keep the human mind occupied, because it cannot stand the silence, the quiet, or inner peace. However, grasping a spiritual message is not an activity of the mind or body, and so it cannot become imbued in our consciousness unless the mind is quiet, peaceful, silent.

This morning as I was in meditation, everything extraneous dropped away from me. It was as though I were in a vacuum; my mind emptied of all thoughts. Then suddenly this message, which I am now giving you, came to me. Because I gave no thought about what I wanted to say, *It* could reveal to me the message I was to impart today. You have to set up a vacuum to make it possible for *It* not only to announce *Itself* but also for it to function as your individual experience.

The voice of God is speaking twenty-four hours a day. *It* has been speaking since the beginning of time. *It* is very much like a twenty-four-hour-a-day radio broadcasting station. But you must become aware of *It* and tune in to *It*; and you could have been tuning in any time in the past year or even ten years! *It* was speaking; *It* was revealing *Itself* in human consciousness. Somewhere on earth others were hearing *It* while we were busy "knitting booties for the grandchild." Let us not be so busy "knitting" that we are not tuning in. But remember that tuning in is not an activity of the mind. The only activity of the mind is in the meditation and contemplation by which we quiet our minds and achieve that stillness in which we hear the Voice. Do not believe that the meditation and contemplation are *It*, because they are not *It* at all. The *It* is the Christ, and Christ announces *Itself* only when we are silent and the mind is quiet.

From Nothingness to Allness

The purpose of turning from material persons, material help, and material avenues to the spiritual is to come to that place in consciousness where the Christ takes over. The moment we turn from the human to the spiritual, it is inevitable that the Spirit will take over. It is just as inevitable as the crop of grass that comes up after the seed is planted, watered, and fertilized. But just as there is an interval between the planting and the reaping, so is there an interval between the first steps you take on the spiritual path and experiencing the Christ activity in your daily life. That interval represents the mess and mass of humanhood that must be cleansed out of the temple of our consciousness because our temples have become soiled with human experience. The Christ *Itself* seems to require some time to purify us—to get this temple (our consciousness) ready for the conception and birth of the Babe.

Regardless of how long ago you turned from the human to the spiritual, no matter how many steps you may have taken (some right and some wrong), it is inevitable that eventually you will come to that place in consciousness where the Christ takes over. But first must come the sense of nothingness, the realization that "nothing I do or think helps; nothing I try to do comes out right." The sense of nothingness: the nothingness of human thought, human self, human being, human action, human wisdom, human planning, human saving—anything human. When the sense of nothingness is complete and we realize the complete futility of human effort and turn to the Spirit, then comes the Allness, the deep silence of "My Peace." That is spiritual peace. "My Presence will never leave you nor forsake you." That is the *I* that is transcendental in nature; *It* is not a human you or me. *It* is the still, small voice that bears witness to the Presence that we will never see face-to-face while living as humans. But when we live as spiritual beings, *It* comes into our experience as it was promised to us.

When It comes, do not make an oddity of yourself to the world. Do not go around telling the world that there is an invisible Presence and Power living your life. Do not tell the world about not taking thought for your life, because the world will become afraid of you and lock you up! But wherever there is a receptive thought, whenever someone comes to you in recognition of what you have, then you can be free to share it. Otherwise, be normal, speak the language of the world, live outwardly the same as everyone else, but inwardly have your spiritual standards you conform to.

My yoke is easy, and my burden is light. [2]

Experiencing the Christ comes only after the death of some part of our humanness, the sloughing off of human self (selfishness), desires, wants, or wishes. As our humanness sloughs off, we rise into the higher state of Christhood. However, no one rises so high that he or she stays there until the moment of ascension, because the transition does not come as long as there is even a trace of humanness left in us. Sometimes the Presence seems to be sitting right on top or in back of your heart or on your shoulder. It may be one place today and another tomorrow. It makes no difference. If you happen to feel it here, there, or some other place, just rejoice! But do not expect it to be there all the time or you will be disappointed. Do not try to localize it or hold on to it or capture it. If it seems to be absent for a long while, it may leave you depressed, but do not be concerned about that either. Life is all hills and valleys. Sometimes you are on a lovely hill, and you slide down into a valley. Other days you are on a mountaintop—higher than Mt. Whitney. I have known the mountaintop feeling to be followed the next day by feeling lower than hell itself. Do not be concerned about it because it has nothing to do with you. It is only the unfolding degrees of consciousness and the human response to them. So if you find yourself in a depressed period, rejoice in that, because it is a preparation for the mountaintop experiences. You cannot go up until you first go down. In other words, you cannot find your life until you lose it.

---

[2]Matthew 11:30.

How can you tell when all sense of humanness has left you? One method never fails. Do you care whether you live or die? If you do care, there is still a trace of humanness. When humanness has left, it makes no difference to you whether you are here on earth or in the hereafter, or whether you are functioning on this plane or the next. Why? When you have sloughed off all trace of humanness, there is no "I" left. Only the human "I" wants to live or sometimes may want to die. It is only the human "I" who can be prosperous or who can lack. If there were no "I," there would be neither prosperity nor lack, neither life nor death, neither sickness nor health. There would be only a state of Christhood. As long as there is a trace of "I," there is humanness.

The burden of human existence will never again be as deep to you after today, because heretofore you have had a sense of "I." "How will I meet this? How shall I meet this? How should I meet this?" But henceforth you will remember, "*I* am with you to meet the problem. *I* will never leave you nor forsake you." Today, something has happened: the Christ realization. *It* will do the doing; *It* will know the knowing; *It* will act the acting; *It* will maintain the maintaining. In other words, there will be a greater sense of the invisible Presence and Power that will perform what is given us to do, and it is for that reason that the burdens will seem smaller. The burdens only seem great when we have to carry them ourselves. The burden is never so great when we know that there is a shoulder to carry it. Christ said, "Come unto me, all ye that labor and are heavy laden, and I will give you rest. . . . And ye shall find rest unto your souls . . . for my yoke is easy, and my burden is light."[3]

Yes, you can rest your burdens on My shoulder. They are no weight on the Christ shoulder at all, not one bit! As Christ makes *Itself* evident in your experience, there will be less of "I" (you) carrying the burden of having to solve a problem and more of *"I, My Presence"* (the Christ) being there to do it for you. After studying, reading, and praying about this, now it is to become your experience!

---

[3]Matthew 11:28–30.